Canadi
from World War I

An Anthology

Edited by Joel Baetz

Milestones in Canadian Literature

OXFORD
UNIVERSITY PRESS

70 Wynford Drive, Don Mills, Ontario M3C 1J9
www.oupcanada.com

Oxford University Press is a department of the University of Oxford. It furthers the University's objective of
excellence in research, scholarship, and education by publishing worldwide in

Oxford   New York
Auckland   Cape Town   Dar es Salaam   Hong Kong   Karachi   Kuala Lumpur   Madrid   Melbourne
Mexico City   Nairobi   New Delhi   Shanghai   Taipei   Toronto

With offices in
Argentina   Austria   Brazil   Chile   Czech Republic   France   Greece   Guatemala   Hungary   Italy   Japan
Poland   Portugal   Singapore   South Korea   Switzerland   Thailand   Turkey   Ukraine   Vietnam

Oxford is a trade mark of Oxford University Press in the UK and in certain other countries

Published in Canada by Oxford University Press

Library and Archives Canada Cataloguing in Publication

Canadian poetry from World War I : an anthology / Joel Baetz, editor.

(Milestones in Canadian literature)
Includes bibliographical references and index.
ISBN 978-0-19-543171-1

1. War poetry, Canadian (English). 2. World War, 1914-1918—Poetry. 3. Canadian poetry
(English)—20th century. I. Baetz, Joel, 1976– II. Series: Milestones in Canadian literature

PS8287.W3B38 2009   C811'.52080358   C2008-907816-0

Cover image: "Kaleidoscope" by Claudia Jean McCabe, SCA.

1 2 3 4 - 12 11 10 09

Oxford University Press is committed to our environment. This book is printed on Forest Stewardship
Council certified paper which contains 100% post-consumer waste. Printed and bound in Canada.

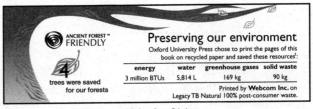

Preserving our environment

Oxford University Press chose to print the pages of this
book on recycled paper and saved these resources[1]:

	energy	water	greenhouse gases	solid waste
	3 million BTUs	5,814 L	169 kg	90 kg

Printed by **Webcom Inc.** on
Legacy TB Natural 100% post-consumer waste.

ANCIENT FOREST™
FRIENDLY

4
trees were saved
for our forests

FSC

Mixed Sources
Product group from well-managed
forests, controlled sources and
recycled wood or fiber

Cert no. SW-COC-002358
www.fsc.org
© 1996 Forest Stewardship Council

[1]Estimates were made using the Environmental Defense Paper Calculator.

"*You will probably be pleased to learn that I have taken up with the muse again: [. . .] a bit of verse [called] 'In Flander's Fields' [sic] will appear in Punch: it's [sic] intention is not jovial.*"
—John McCrae, diary entry of 14 November 1915

Canadians were passionate about World War I from the very beginning to its closing moments. Over 600,000 soldiers signed up for the fight, and those who stayed at home looked almost everywhere for news about the events in Europe. Some trusted the eyewitness accounts published in our newspapers, some held out hope for a letter from a loved one, and thousands of Canadians turned to poetry.

Until now, Canadian poetry about the war has been overlooked. We all know John McCrae's "In Flanders Fields," but there are other poets that deserve our attention. Almost every poet of the period wrote about the war—from Charles G.D. Roberts to A.J.M. Smith, from Helena Coleman to Frank Prewett to Robert Service. Their works appear here in the first anthology solely devoted to Canadian war poetry, helping us to remember—or see for the first time—the war's soaring emotions, complex ideas, and lasting impacts.

For Rodelyn

Contents

Acknowledgements   ix
Introduction: Beyond Flanders Fields   1
A Note on the Text   16

Anna Durie   17
    A Bugle Call   18
    At Home   20
    The Daily Letter   21
    My Heart It Is a Shrine for Deeds of His   21
    Passchendaele   22
    Requiem   28
    A Soldier's Grave in France   29
    Sunrise in France   29
    Vimy Ridge   30

William Wilfred Campbell   34
    The Summons   35
    Our Dead   37
    The Fight Goes On   38
    Langemarck   39

Helena Coleman   44
    Challenge   45
    Convocation Hall   47
    The Day He Went   47
    Marching Men   48
    O, Not When April Wakes the Daffodils   50
    Pro Patria Mortui   51
    The Recruit   52
    'Tis Not the Will That's Wanted   52
    When First He Put the Khaki On   53

Charles G.D. Roberts   55
   Cambrai and Marne   56
   Going Over   58

Frederick George Scott   59
   A Canadian   60
   A Grave in Flanders   61
   Requiescant   62

Duncan Campbell Scott   63
   Somewhere in France   64
   To a Canadian Aviator Who Died for His Country in France   67
   To a Canadian Lad Killed in the War   68
   To the Canadian Mothers   69

John Daniel Logan   72
   Renouncement   73
   Timor Mortis   74
   Farewell to France   76
   The Immortal Bonds   77
   Night Witchery in France   78

John McCrae   80
   The Anxious Dead   81
   In Flanders Fields   81

Robert Service   83
   The Call   84
   The Fool   85
   Foreword   87
   On the Wire   89
   The Revelation   91
   The Stretcher-Bearer   94

F.O. Call   95
   Calvary   96
   In a Belgian Garden   96
   The Indifferent Ones   97
   The Lace-Maker of Bruges   98

Gone West   98
To a Modern Poet   99

Katherine Hale   101
Grey Knitting   102
When You Return   103
You Who Have Gayly Left Us   103
The Awakening   104
The Hearts of Mothers   105
Soul of the Earth   106

Wilson MacDonald   108
The Girl Behind the Man Behind the Gun   108

E.J. Pratt   111
Dead on the Field of Honour   112
The Largess of 1917   112
Before a Bulletin Board   115
From A Fragment from a Story   115

Douglas Leader Durkin   121
The Call   122
Carry On!   123
The Father Speaks   124
The Fighting Men of Canada   127
Good-Byes, a la Mode   129
The Men Who Stood   131
The Monument   132

Albert William Drummond   133
The Battlefield   133
The Colonial's Challenge   136
The Empire   137
On the Banks of the Somme   138
The Stretcher-Bearers   139

Bernard Freeman Trotter   141
A Canadian Twilight   142
Dreams   144

"*Ici Repose*"   145
The Poplars   147

Frank Prewett   149
    Burial Stones   150
    Card Game   151
    The Soldier   151
    Soliloquy   152
    The Survivor   153

A.J.M. Smith   154
    A Soldier's Ghost   155

Appendices
    Appendix A: Canadian Authors Writing about World War I   156
    Frank Prewett, "Letters"   156
    John Daniel Logan, "The Fatal Paradox and Sin of Sorrow for the
    Dead"   159
    From Robert Service, *Records of a Red Cross Man*   161
    Peregrine Acland, "Thoughts of a Returned Soldier"   170

    Appendix B: Canadian Authors Writing about World War I
    Poetry   174
    John Ridington, *The Poetry of the War*   174
    John Daniel Logan, Preface to *The New Apocalypse and Other
    Poems of Days and Deeds in France*   178
    From Frederick George Scott, *The Great War As I Saw It*   182

    Appendix C: Perspectives on Canadian War Art: A Case Study   185
    Paul Konody, "On War Memorials"   186
    Anonymous, "War's Spirit in Painters' Colors"   189
    Anonymous, "More Shocks in Store for Ordinary Folk at 'Ex' Art
    Gallery"   191

Sources   195
Credits   197

Acknowledgements

Thank you to John Lennox, Jonathan Warren, David Bentley, Brian Trehearne, and Kevin Flynn, who have all made this anthology, my other scholarly work, and my teaching more thorough, cogent, and ambitious. From my first essay as an undergraduate to this current project, they have given me the kind of help for which any young scholar hopes. Thank you also to Jennie Rubio, who showed immediate enthusiasm for the work and guided the project with an eager and patient hand. Thank you to Katie Scott for her keen editorial eye and helpful suggestions. Thank you to Dave Milman for his painstaking but valuable work.

Thank you to my parents, Stephen and Marilyn, for their constant love and encouragement, their creativity and determination, and their impossibly good examples. Everyone should be so lucky. Thank you to Matthew and Alissa for their joy, their interest, and their love. Thank you to Al, Stephanie, Andy, and Charlie, whose Friday night dinners are a welcome break after a long week. Finally, thank you to Rodelyn, whose own work reminds me of the possibility of a better world, and whose love encourages me to be a better person.

The Great War is over—the world's agony has ended. What has been born? The next generation may be able to answer.

—L.M. Montgomery, 11 November 1918

Introduction:
Beyond Flanders Fields

For a long time, the only Canadian poem from World War I that I knew was John McCrae's "In Flanders Fields." Every year I heard it at my school's Remembrance Day ceremony in our small and sweaty gymnasium. Sometimes the principal would read it to us. Sometimes we would read it together, a couple hundred children and a handful of teachers drifting through McCrae's poem about a war that seemed so far away and so long ago. When I was eleven, my teacher asked me to recite it at one of those ceremonies. I learned the poem as best I could, trying to understand its variant meanings and looking for a way to convey its emotional register.

My attachment to that poem remains strong. I can still recite it by memory. But some years ago, I began to wonder about other Canadian poems from World War I. As a graduate student and then as a full-time scholar, I started searching for poems beyond "In Flanders Fields." What I discovered was surprising. Over a hundred Canadians published poetry about the war in local newspapers, collections of their work, and anthologies compiled for charities. As Canadians rushed to recruiting offices and railway platforms to celebrate the latest soldier to join the war or to mourn the latest to die in it, our poets rushed to their desks and notebooks, eager to discover and share what they thought about the origins, participants, and aftermath of the war. For most of these writers, poetry was a public register of emotions and ideas; for a rare few, it was a private record of personal torment.

Whether public or private, poetry was one of the best ways to make sense of the war. In 1917, University of British Columbia librarian John Ridington described the importance of the war poetry this way:

Confronted by Armageddon, with personal, social, national, racial ideals of liberty imperilled, men think deeply, feel acutely, react powerfully. It would be unthinkable that this reaction should not find vent in poetry, the most permanent of all the great avenues of human expression.[1]

*   *   *

When historians talk about Canada's response to the Great War, they usually point to the outpourings of enthusiastic support. They mention the large crowds at public send-offs or memorials, the success of the recruiting efforts, the passionate defences of the war by politicians in Ottawa. And they often tell stories about men like Frederick George Scott.

In the summer of 1914, just days before Britain declared war on Germany, Scott headed over to the newspaper office to catch the latest reports about the mounting tensions in Europe. As the evening's news rolled in about Canada's possible contributions to the war, Scott stood in a crowd of excited townspeople and felt a sudden sense of obligation to serve his country. His autobiography describes that decisive moment: "One after another the reports were given," he writes, "and at last there flashed upon the board the words, 'General Hughes offers a force of twenty thousand men to England in case war is declared against Germany.' I turned to a friend and said, 'That means that I have got to go to the war.'"[2]

Scott was passionate about fulfilling his newly discovered sense of national obligation, but he had concerns, too. It meant leaving the ordinary comforts of home; it meant encountering dangers he could not yet imagine or that he had only read about in books. But Scott enlisted anyway. He served for four years, saw men injured beyond recognition, held funerals for the dead (those killed by the enemy and those who took their own lives), and witnessed a period in western history that he would eventually call "a nightmare."[3] And yet one of

[1]   John Ridington, "The Poetry of the War: An Address Delivered Before the Pacific Northwest Library Association at the Public Library, Portland, Oregon" (UBC Archives: n.p. [1918]), 4.
[2]   Frederick George Scott, *The Great War As I Saw It* (Toronto: Goodchild, 1922), 15.
[3]   Scott, *Great War*, 317.

the remarkable things about Scott—and so many other Canadians—is that nothing could shake his devotion to the war, his sense of purpose, and his admiration for the men who fought. By the end of his autobiography, the war remains "the great adventure of my life among the most glorious men that the world has ever produced."[4]

Scott's enthusiasm for the war—its duration, its intensity, and even its limits—was typical. Canadians were by and large fervent supporters of the war effort, from its very beginning until its final moments—even as they realized the extent of the violence and the number of dead.[5] Recruiting offices and railway platforms were jammed with men eager for the fight and well-wishers sending them on their way. Newspapers were crammed with stories, editorials, and advertisements about the war. Crowds gathered on sidewalks to discuss the latest news or rumours about the events in Europe. Sermons and speeches by preachers and politicians were packed with arguments about the value of patriotism and the lofty ideals of duty, sacrifice, and nobility.

Canada's enthusiasm for the war is well known; histories of our war efforts almost always mention it. What is less well known, however, is that this enthusiasm was accompanied by a soaring interest in writing and reading about the war. Scott himself was both a willing soldier and an avid writer, creating a mournful and solemn book of poems about his own wartime experiences as well as a tense autobiography. And he wasn't the only one. Canadian soldiers eagerly enlisted for active duty and wrote about their lives overseas; those back home were equally eager to read apparently objective records of the battles, sanitized descriptions of trench life, impassioned claims about the moral righteousness of the war, and fictional and poetic accounts of life at the front.

And there was plenty of material available. Since the mid-nineteenth century, the Canadian publishing industry had under-gone a series of changes that made it easier to produce and sell books.

---

[4] Scott, *Great War*, 317.
[5] Over six hundred thousand Canadians joined the war in Europe; more than a third of them were wounded or killed.

The industrial revolution made production more efficient and materials cheaper. The expansion and development of modes of transportation and infrastructure improved distribution. At the same time, the rise in literacy rates, the popularity of book clubs, and the increased number of libraries meant readers were more plentiful and more passionate.[6] It was, according to Clarence Karr, a golden age for Canadian publishing.[7]

By 1914 the publishing boom was in full swing, producing a steady supply of books about the war for a new and untapped market. The bookselling industry's trade magazines claimed that patriotic war books would bring in steady and loyal customers. Current affairs periodicals reported on the new and crucial role of Canadian libraries during the war or discussed the steady increase in war literature of all kinds; there were at least, one article estimated, "one thousand different war books, all of which have had sales varying from one hundred only to twenty-five, thirty, forty thousand."[8] Newspapers themselves were packed with ads and reviews promoting war literature. The 5 December 1917 edition of *The Globe*, for instance, offered a full-page promotion of war literature. Flanked by advertisements that point out "Some Good War Books," the centre columns review "The Season's Best Books"—most of which are also about the war, including Bernard Freeman Trotter's *A Canadian Twilight*, Helena Coleman's *Marching Men*, and Ralph Connor's *The Major*.

The arrival of Canadian war literature did not go unnoticed. For the earliest scholars of Canadian literature the war was a crucial event, galvanizing poets with a common cause and inspiring a new kind of poetry—something that had not happened since Confederation. In his presidential address to the Royal Society of Canada in 1918, W.D. Lighthall described the significance of war for our country and our literature. "The Great War," argued Lighthall, "is

---

[6]   George L. Parker, "The Evolution of Publishing in Canada," *The History of the Book in Canada*, vol. 2 (Toronto: University of Toronto Press, 2005), 17–32.

[7]   Clarence Karr, *Authors and Audiences: Popular Canadian Fiction in the Early Twentieth Century* (Montreal: McGill-Queens University Press, 2000).

[8]   Hugh Eayrs, "Canadian Publishers and War Propaganda," *Canadian Bookman*, January 19, 49.

vastly more stirring as an era than Confederation was," and "must be regarded as a new starting point" for Canadian literature.[9] Two years earlier John Daniel Logan—soldier, poet, and literary historian—had made a similar point:

> The flowering of the poetic spirit on the fighting field has, by admiration and emulation, not only stimulated the general poetic spirit but also caused it to disclose its existence and potency in a new generation of poets of nature, society and the arts of peace. In a phrase, the Great War has created an authentic Renascence[10] of the Poetic Spirit and of Poetry.[11]

Logan and Lighthall were right. Canadian war poetry is remarkable—but not for the reasons that they imagined. They both admired war poetry for its romantic features and firm moral stance. In their estimations, the war inspired a specific kind of poetry of grand abstractions, great adventures, and clear lessons in honour and virtue. For Lighthall this poetry was distinctive for its "Supreme heroism," "Ideals of fidelity," and "Hatred of Wrong."[12] Similarly, Logan described how Canada's "soldier-poets sang of truth for their own comfort, solace, strengthening and joy in noble doing."[13]

If we move beyond the narrow interests of Logan's and Lighthall's bold claims, we can still discover the impressiveness of the period's literature. A closer look nearly a century later reveals the vibrancy and intensity of the period, its ideological commitments, its quiet disputes about the form, function, and subjects of poetry. This poetry is nothing less than a culturally informed archive of ideas; it is a warehouse of thoughts and emotions about an extraordinary range of topics, including strength, race, community, obligation, gender, vulnerability, truth, obscurity, trauma, and death.

---

[9]   W.D. Lighthall, *Canadian Poets of the Great War: Presidential Address* (Ottawa: Royal Society of Canada, 1918), 16.

[10] rebirth; also a period of literary history from 1500–1660 in England (Abrams)

[11] John Daniel Logan, preface to *The New Apocalypse and Other Poems of Days and Deeds in France* (Halifax: T.C. Allen, 1919), xi.

[12] Lightball, *Canadian Poets*, 16.

[13] Logan, preface to *New Apocalypse*, xi.

The recognition of poetry's formal and thematic diversity would
be a much-needed dismissal of Logan's and Lighthall's initial inter-
pretations, and a necessary expansion of two more recent arguments
about World War I poetry. The first is from historian Jonathan F.
Vance's *Death So Noble*, which reminds us that war was seen as the
"progenitor of good" in Canada.[14] The poetry is both traditional and
enthusiastic, Vance argues, in order to make the war seem "familiar
and non-threatening." The second comes from Paul Fussell's *The
Great War and Modern Memory*. Here Fussell marshals evidence—
gleaned in large part from the poetry by the likes of Siegfried Sassoon
and Wilfred Owen—to conclude that the war produced "one domi-
nating form of modern understanding; that it is essentially ironic."[15]
Given the grim realities of the war, the uplifting sentiment and grand
abstractions of the patriotic war poetry and propaganda could, in the
end, be only ironic or misleading. The war, in Fussell's estimation,
was not the progenitor of good; it was the source of alienation,
obscurity, and limitation.

Both arguments are seminal, powerful, and useful—to a degree.
They highlight broad cultural patterns. That is the business of
writing about social memory or cultural history. Their conclusions
are generally true, but they ignore the idiosyncratic poets and
poems that lie outside their argument's well-defined boundaries.
One of the tasks of this anthology, then, is to both complement and
challenge Vance's and Fussell's sweeping interpretations. This
collection shows that the poetry is more than a one-note song, more
than a simple and enthusiastic hurrah for the war or a collective and
cathartic moan in the face of devastation. Those enthusiastic
hurrahs are fascinating for their expansive register of ideas, their
rhetorical force, and their supreme confidence. Those collective and
cathartic moans are intriguing for the ways in which they convey
emotion and achieve some modicum of consolation. And the

---

[14] Jonathan F. Vance, *Death So Noble: Memory, Meaning, and the First World War* (Vancouver: UBC Press, 1997), 11.
[15] Paul Fussell, *The Great War and Modern Memory*, 2nd ed. (Toronto: Oxford University Press, 2000), 35.

poems that fit neither mould—the modernist renditions of death and pessimism, for instance—invite our attention, point us to different ways of understanding the war, and repay our interpretative efforts.

There is no denying that the interpretations of Logan, Lighthall, Vance, and Fussell can explain many of the characteristics of the poetry of World War I. But there is a great deal of additional complexity in this poetry well worth exploring. To facilitate the recognition of some of the often overlooked ideas in our World War I poetry, the following pages will highlight four of its more dominant features: its focus on communal strength and personal torment; the tension between clarity and obscurity; the differences between men and women; and the meaning of the dead.

Communal Strength and Personal Torment

One of this poetry's most conspicuous features is its emphasis on collective action. While that alone may not be surprising, its frequency is. From the very beginning, the war was framed by politicians, historians, and citizens as a communal event that would bring together citizens from different classes and parts of the country to form a single-minded military unit. The idealized image of the Canadian soldier, that rugged and stalwart hero that appeared on recruiting posters and in news reports, was a manifestation of this emphasis on collectivity. He was the embodiment of an entire nation, evidence that the diversity of Canada could be summed up in the dashing figure of a single soldier.

The poetry's emphasis on collectivity is obvious. It is very often a poetry about crowds, about the power of a "we" and the hopelessness of an "I," about uniform groups of uniformed men, and about organized collective action. In the poetry, this celebration of strong and unified communities usually takes one of two forms: the dramatization of the assembly or successful effort of a military group, or the insistence that a single soldier embodies an entire nation. The former strategy shows itself in Albert William Drummond's "The Colonial's

Challenge"; we can see the latter in Douglas Leader Durkin's "The Men Who Stood."

For the most part, English-Canadian poetry from World War I expends considerable effort sealing off the gaps between disparate geographies and people. It masks the differences between home front and front line, soldier and citizen, the living and the dead. But on occasion, these gaps and differences are more noticeable. Robert Service's poetry is equally enthusiastic about and suspicious of collective action. "The Volunteer" recognizes the difference between the speaker's own desires and those of "[t]hem empire-grabbers," yet the soldier eventually enlists. Helena Coleman's poetry also strikes an ambivalent note. "Marching Men" admires the power of the "thousands strong" with "Pride of country, pride of race / Glowing in each ruddy face." But "When First He Put the Khaki On" focuses on the jarring disconnect between the soldier's uniform—a sign of maturity and manliness—and the "child [who] looked out / … / Beneath the man's disguise."

Censorship, Realism, and the War

The sheer distance from the battlefields of Europe was one of the main reasons that Canadians knew very little about events on the front lines. That distance allowed censors to keep a close eye on the information coming from France, London, or Belgium. Despite the nearly insatiable desire for information about their fellow citizens, friends, or family members, Canadians only had access to the heavily censored reports that appeared in the newspapers or the blacked-out letters that arrived from the front. Unlike the British, who had easier access to information about front line conditions from soldiers on leave, most Canadians were left with doubly censored material—once at the front and once at home.[16]

---

[16] Jeffrey A. Keshen, *Propaganda and Censorship During Canada's Great War* (Edmonton: University of Alberta Press, 1996).

The result of such heavy censorship was that most Canadians did not question the heroism and virtue of Canadian soldiers, the strength of the British Empire, and the brazen wickedness of the German forces. Any account that tested the laws of censorship was either dismissed as untrue or offensive, or in a few rare cases, celebrated as a faithful and factual account of what was happening all the way across the Atlantic.

The best examples of these attitudes are the responses to Robert Service's *Rhymes of a Red Cross Man*. Service had previously published reports of his experience as an ambulance driver in newspapers in Ottawa, Montreal, and Toronto, and had been criticized by chief censor Lieutenant-Colonel Ernest J. Chambers. But his *Rhymes of a Red Cross Man*—a mix of battle romance and violent images—garnered a more complex reaction from readers. To a social conservative like Logan, the collection of poetry was nothing but "versified brutalities, or poetical garbage."[17] But to many Canadians, it offered a much-needed honesty. For two years, it was a best-seller in the non-fiction category.

By the mid-point of the war, there was growing suspicion of the censored accounts. Sir Max Aitken's official (and flawed) reports from the front appeared in newspapers as eyewitness reports, but they were no better than what had already been dismissed in England as eyewash. As early as 1915, soldiers and citizens were well aware of the misleading nature of the news reports. In his diary, John McCrae writes about laughable inaccuracies of the Montreal and Toronto papers. In *Maclean's*, Lieutenant-Colonel John Bayne Maclean wrote that British and Canadian Governments were "suppressing the truth" and that "actual war conditions have been persistently misreported to us."[18]

In the poetry, the ability to accurately represent the experience of the front lines waxes and wanes. The majority of the poems were written and read as though they offered faithful depictions of the war.

---

[17] John Daniel Logan, "Canadian Poetry of the Great War," *Canadian Magazine*, March 1917, 412.
[18] John McCrae, diary entry of 31 May 1915 (MG 30, D 209, John McCrae Collection, Library and Archives Canada). John Bayne Maclean, "Suppressing the Truth," *Maclean's*, April 1918, 45.

F.O. Call and Douglas Leader Durkin could only imagine what happened on the front lines, but that did not stop them from writing about it in "Gone West" and "The Men Who Stood." Anna Durie followed her son to London and France and spoke with him often about the war, but "Vimy Ridge" could only be based on second-hand information from her son, friends, and newspapers—something that the poem itself makes clear. These poems, like so many others, are confident in their ability to know and convey what it was like to fight and die on the front lines.

A few poems are more challenging, focussing on the problems of clear and direct knowledge. On these occasions, the front is a strange and unknowable territory and soldiers are inscrutable and obscure men. In Service's "The Odyssey of 'Erbert 'Iggins," for instance, the war is an event that defies terms like "reality" or "fact"; it is only a strange event, most real when it looks like a movie.

Fighting Men, Crying Women

Addressing the Women's Canadian Club in September 1917, convalescing soldier Peregrine Acland reminded his audience what was at stake in the war. Here was a chance to defend democracy, to aim for a higher purpose, to embark on a grand adventure, to live a life of "infinite wonder, whose very terrors [enhance] its beauties." Acland went on to say that war was a chance to achieve a rare and lofty kind of manliness. "[T]o fight well in any cause that seems good," he intoned, "is as much as can be expected of man."[19]

The idea that war is a "manly enterprise" was a popular one in the early twentieth century and appeared in everything from politician's speeches to recruiting posters to patriotic poetry. This poetry defines and defends war as a masculine pursuit, as a way to become an honourable, noble, and strong man. The relationship between the

---

[19]   Peregrine Acland, "Thoughts of a Returned Soldier," *The Rebel*, December 1917, 98–99.

virile and virtuous is durable and appears with surprising frequency, celebrating the soldier as an emblem of bodily and spiritual strength. But women have a different fate. For the most part, the women in these poems (aside from the personified Mother England) have one function: to remind readers of war's devastating losses and its emotional toll. These textual women are vehicles for concern and anxiety; they give voice to sadness and dread and act as textual signs of war's horrific consequences. And when their restlessness is stayed, their anxieties eased, their sadness resolved, and their concerns dismissed or overcome, the poems remind us (or try to) that war is worthwhile, its costs manageable and deaths heroic.

There is no doubt that World War I provided some Canadian women the opportunity to consider new identities—worker, for instance—that had been less accessible before the men left to fight. But the bulk of the war's poetry rarely pays attention to these new opportunities. Sandra Gilbert and Susan Gubar's *No Man's Land* makes a point about British culture during World War I that is, at least in part, applicable to Canada. The war meant an "apocalypse for masculinism" and "an apotheosis of femaleness." As men experienced alienation, trauma, and fractiousness, women experienced the thrill of possibility as "nurses, as mistresses, as munitions workers."[20] Yet relatively little Canadian poetry explores these new possibilities for women. Most of it keeps women in their role as markers of loss and separation, reservoirs of emotional turmoil that are, on occasion, easily quieted.

So, there is a double edge to poems like Duncan Campbell Scott's "To Canadian Mothers" and Wilson MacDonald's "The Girl Behind the Man Behind the Gun." They examine women's wartime experiences—how they mourn and survive personal tragedy. But the poems restrict the war's potential to redefine gender roles; there is no apotheosis of feminism here, no liberating energy for women.

[20] Sandra Gilbert and Susan Gubar, *No Man's Land*, vol. 2 (New Haven: Yale University Press, 1989), 262–263.

We Are the Dead

John McCrae's "In Flanders Fields" is the most popular poem from World War I. Appearing first in the British magazine *Punch* in December 1915, the poem quickly became famous. Yet it had little impact on Canadian poetry. It inspired a few responses, some poetic, some musical, but nothing remarkable. Far more significant was a poem by British poet Rupert Brooke. A leading figure of England's Georgian poetry movement, Brooke entered the war with romantic intentions but died before he saw battle. Mere days before his death, Brooke wrote a series of five sonnets, two of which deserve special mention. The first, titled "Peace," encouraged readers to leap into action; war was a chance to fight off the cultural malaise that had overtaken England and an opportunity to regain past glories. The last and most famous sonnet, called "The Soldier," strikes a different note. It begins:

> If I should die, think only this of me:
> That there's some corner of a foreign field
> That is for ever England. There shall be
> In that rich earth a richer dust concealed[.]

In England, those words were read by Dean Inge in St. Paul's Cathedral on Easter Sunday in 1915, and provided citizens with a degree of comfort and confidence, born of two distinct but related features: a strident faith in the durability and significance of the British Empire; and an insistence on the power of the mourning, or literally the "thinking," that is mentioned in the poem's first line. The dead—no matter how far away—would always be English. That so-called dust would always be part of a larger English body, connected to the lively and mournful citizens back home.

In Canada, Brooke's poem had a massive impact. Like Logan, some poets invoke Brooke directly, praise him for his work, dedicate poems to him, or allude to the lines from his fifth sonnet that are quoted above. Other poems—such as "Our Absent Hero" or "My Heart It Is a Shrine for Deeds of His" by Anna Durie, "The Soldier" by Frank Prewett, or "A Soldier's Ghost" by A.J.M. Smith—have a different and more oblique relationship with Brooke's fifth sonnet. The image of the "Bones / distilled in the frontier sand" that appears in Smith's poem can be understood as a powerful revision of the opening images of Brooke's poem, only Smith's bones have an uneasy relationship with the signs of military participation. They merely "fumble / The natty chevron"; in Brooke's poem, the dust is an immediate sign of England's scope and strength.

*   *   *

There are, of course, other noteworthy features of English-Canadian war poetry that warrant mention: the use of Christian images and ideas; the form and function of violence; the occasional appearance of trauma; the degree of formal control; the coincidence of race and nation; the images of nature as indices of national health; and the shifting demands of the epic and the lyric. I have tried to avoid approaching these poems in the way so many readers have before, treating them as simple (or overly simplistic) paeans to Canada and its people. When that happens, the poetry becomes easily dismissible by our contemporary and scholarly interpretations of nation, war, and violence.

What is at stake here is a more complex understanding of a crucial part of our cultural and, more specifically, literary history. Historians have been treating World War I with admirable sophistication for years. They have challenged the easy and attractive—but ultimately misleading—reputations of the war and have made room for more complicated understandings. Canadian novelists have done something similar. Writers as varied as Ralph Connor, Charles Yale Harrison, Hugh MacLennan, Timothy Findley, Frances Itani, and Joseph Boyden have been documenting and interpreting the war since it began, confirming or shifting its popular meanings and aftermaths.

Yet when it comes to our war poetry, we have only a broad and simplistic understanding of it. It is an understanding that first took shape in Logan's and Lighthall's commentaries and has been repeated in the histories of our literature that dismiss or overlook it. It is an understanding that has led us to believe that McCrae's poem is the only one worth remembering. It is an understanding that has led to the dismissal of the war poetry from anthologies of Canadian literature. The poems collected here should preserve and expand that reputation by allowing readers to acknowledge its emotional force and its expansive roster of immense and intricate ideas.

The diversity of the poetry should remind us to be wary of fast and firm lines of division. There is no absolute difference between the poetry of soldier-poets and home-front citizens. Soldiers are just as likely to write patriotic epics as poets back in Canada. Nor does August 1914 act as a dividing line, separating romance from modernism, illusion from reality, or sincerity from irony. Literary history is always more complicated than at first glance, and the poetry written during and about World War I is no different. Granted, there are some general patterns that are worth keeping in mind. A soldier's poetry is more likely to describe the blood and violence of the front than a citizen's poetry. A younger poet is more likely to entertain modernist topics and styles than an older poet. But even these general patterns all have their exceptions.

To illuminate the diversity and significance of the period, this anthology offers a selection of poems chosen according to the following criteria: the quality of the poetry; the significance of the poet in Canadian literary history; the number of war poems written by the poet; and how the poetry complements or differs from other poetry in the collection. Of all the criteria, the first is the hardest to defend or explain. Taste is fickle and personal. Whenever I describe my current research interests, people inevitably ask, "But is it good poetry?" Every time my answer is the same: "It's always interesting." The poetry is fascinating for its emotional depth, intriguing for its ideological complexity, and important for the way in which it challenges our understanding of Canadian literary history.

We have a lot to learn about our English-Canadian poetry from World War I; we also have a lot to learn from it. Its lessons about the conditions and aftermath of war are applicable to the wars that dominate our news today. In fact, as a culture we are continuing to perform the wartime rituals of enthusiasm and mourning that were so popular during World War I. Military officials, journalists, and politicians urge us to see the potential costs and rewards of fighting in Iraq or Afghanistan, and ask us to remember the bravery of our soldiers. People still gather to watch the dead return from faraway battlefields. We're asked to make sacrifices, albeit more modest than those made in World War I; we're told that our national reputation depends on it; we're advised that civilization hangs in the balance.

When we turn to this poetry, it should tell us about the unique features of World War I and the way our poets saw it; the war's greatness lies in its inventions, in its scope, in its number of heroes and casualties, and in the cultural products that were and still remain fascinated by it. But the poetry can also tell us something about the world that we live in. One of the great values of literature is its unparalleled capacity to teach us about the historical circumstances that made it possible and the current conditions in which it is read. In particular, since we live in a world that is so involved in international armed conflict, this collection of English-Canadian war poetry should help us consider the inevitable versions of heroism, injury, national obligation, violence, and death that we hear almost daily. This poetry should help us to remember—or see for the first time—the durability and consequences of the ideas that it articulated, defended, and attacked as it drew its own battle lines.

A Note on the Text

These poems have been transcribed from their original appearance in book form. Obvious errors have been silently corrected.

Poets are arranged chronologically, by date of birth; poems are arranged by original date of publication. On occasion (especially when the date of publication is more than ten years later than its composition), the date of composition appears in italics at the end of the poem.

Anna Durie

(1856–1933)

When Anna Durie's son, William, left for war, she quickly followed. A bank clerk in Toronto, William was called to service in 1915, became a member of the 58th Battalion as a musketry officer, and arrived at the front in March 1916. By then, Durie had been in London for almost a year.

At home and abroad, Durie went to extraordinary lengths to protect her son. She urged William's fellow officers to watch out for him, petitioned government officials to allow her to follow her son to the Western Front, and when he was injured, begged him to stay away from the lines. Even after a punctured lung, a medical assessment that he was "likely to die," and a diagnosis of "neurasthenia" (what we now know as shell shock), he longed to return. He went back to the trenches, was eventually promoted to Captain, and died in a shelling barrage near the end of the Battle of Passchendaele. Although barred by law to remove her son from his grave in France, Durie successfully smuggled her son's remains home. Both mother and son are buried in adjacent plots in St. James Cemetery in Toronto.[1]

Frequently reminiscent of Rupert Brooke's "The Soldier," Durie's elegies speak about the depth of her grief and her desire to retain and rehabilitate her understanding of her son's actions.

A Bugle Call

Give me back the years of wonder,
   Bring again the days of war!
Let me feel my pulses throbbing,
Close my ears to children's sobbing,
And my life of sorrow robbing,
   Take away the days that are.
      Give me back the years of wonder,
      Bring again the days of war!

Let me hear the tramp of soldiers,
   Sound again the bugle call!   10
Break the quiet of my gloaming[2]
With the noise of waters foaming,
Rushed through chasm and gorge, e'er homing
   Near the camp where heroes dwell.
      Make me hear the songs of soldiers
      Rising clear, from cot and hall.

Days when life was still before us,
   Filled with all that Death could lure;
When our sires and sons proved true men,
With red blood; the shirkers few men;   20

---

[1] For a complete account of Anna and William's war years, see Veronica Cusack, *The Invisible Soldier* (Toronto: McClelland & Stewart, 2004).
[2] evening twilight

When the nation's trumpet drew men
  To resist a common foe.
    Days when honour urged and tore us,
    Days when only death was sure.

Then we saw them in their splendour,
  Caught their hands when lips were dumb.
Take away my grief and trouble,
Give me wheat, nor leave the stubble,
For my sorrow, give me double,
  Far remove the stains of war.   30
    Tell about the Great Surrender;
    Call the years that are to come!

Let me hear their names a-chiming
  In the temple towers of Time!
Show them slain, but crowned victorious,
'Midst a nation's shouts uproarious;
Let me see the Vision Glorious
  Of the years that are to come.
    Show an empire's poets rhyming
    Manhood shattered in its prime.   40

Bring our marching men before me,
  Curb my pride and check my tears.
In the halls of fame and glory,
Grave their names and tell their story,
Till their monuments are hoary[3]
  With the dust of coming years.
    Bring our marching men before me,
    Crown with peace my hopes and fears.

---

[3] grey or greyish white

Own their greatness, life's attraction;
    Set the gates of fame ajar!   50
That sweet youth and poets dreaming,
Touched, may see the glory streaming,
See the splendour, softly gleaming,
    In the vacant years to come.
      Follow them in word and action:
      Nor let slip the dogs of war.

          (1920)

At Home

Your grave shall be a shrine where children come
To leave sweet-scented flowers; where men, being moved,
Shall read, inscribed, your valiant deeds, and sum
Them up and say, "This man a soldier proved."
Your pillow, blue with hyacinths in spring,
Shall fill the air with fragrance, through the years;
When lark and chirping birdlings are a-wing
Women shall read your triumphs through their tears.

You are not dead, tho' loving hands shall come
To touch your grave, and summer rains shall stream   10
From softly weeping skies: you have reached home;
The verdure[4] on your grave shall richly gleam;
But you have winged your way across the foam:
Have slumbered, then awakened from your dream.

          (1920)

---

[4] green or green vegetation

The Daily Letter

Your daily letter from the front! It came,
A message sweet and sacred, telling me
You lived, O heart of mine! How blest to see
The dear, familiar lines, when battle's flame
Was past; to know you safe and just the same!
And every precious letter headed free,
"On active service," brought an ecstasy
Of hope and longing, blent with dreams of fame.

Your daily letter from the front! This said …
No, no! It could not be that you were dead!   10
This sent me all the love you had! said you
Were moving up the line; and dear and true
To the last you wrote. But when your letter came
You'd left the line: and an immortal name.

(1920)

My Heart It Is a Shrine for Deeds of His

My heart it is a shrine for deeds of his
    That live for ever in an ambient light;
Like purest marble that illumined is,
    Or rarest jewels in a casket white.

As falls the sun on shaded chapel wall,
    So streams the radiance of his gallant deeds,
Across the midnight of my life's black pall,
    Shadow by shadow lifting where it leads.

I count my store: set this or that aside,
    Like glittering gems, too precious to be worn: 10
This had its birth in Flanders: ere he died,
    This proved a herald of the approaching morn.

And if I inward turn my thoughts into
   The deeper recess where his image lives,
Set in a sparkling frame of sapphire hue
   That to the deep-set eyes a lustre gives.

Meseems I taste a fragrance in the air,
   A breath that hovers sweet where sunshine is:
A living thing, that comforts like a prayer,
   This heart, that is a shrine for deeds of his.   20

                    (1920)

Passchendaele[5]
October 26th, 1917

Requiem aeternam dona eis, Domine.[6]
(The 58th Battalion, C.E.F., was the first Canadian battalion to
attack at Passchendaele.)

My absent hero, ere himself was laid
To rest, in France, to the requiem[7] of the guns,
On that black day that made the world for me
A sunless place, told, how at Passchendaele
Our troops advanced and took and held the Ridge.

---

[5] Passchendaele is the location of a particularly difficult, devastating—but ultimately successful—battle in Belgium during the late summer and fall of 1917. More than 15,000 Canadian soldiers were killed, but Canadian forces were instrumental in the eventual victory. As a prefatory note to her collection of poetry, *Our Absent Hero*, Durie mentions her son's actions during that battle: "On the evening of October 26, 1917, during the attack at Passchendaele, after heavy fighting throughout the day, he went five times through drum-fire to save the wounded, who had lain since the early morning on the field: an incident that will be for ever associated with his name. No eulogy of his life would be complete that did not place emphasis on his fearlessness in action, his devotion to duty and his gallantry in the field" (v).

[6] "Grant them eternal rest, Lord" (Latin); a line from the Roman Catholic mass for the dead.

[7] Specifically, the Roman Catholic mass for the dead; generally, any song on the occasion of a burial.

I pray you for an instant follow me
In thought to Flanders; take at Ypres a train
And push towards the east; then make descent,
After a twenty minutes' run by rail,
Then take the road, and stand and laugh to scorn   10
The shell-holes on the Ridge, remembering well
That every pockmark meant a human life.
Look down; now throw your swimming eyes across
The path of glory stretching to the east.
For here it was the 58th was given
By luck, the post of honour in the attack
At Passchendaele, the fight, that brought us all
An everlasting fame, and made us great
And more than glorious, at a staggering cost.
Now, thread your way between the humps and scars   20
And you will come, in time, to Bellevue Spur,[8]
Rather, let's say, to the enchanted ground,
Where the old battalion, plunging up the slope,
Tho' met with withering fire from the Huns,[9]
Swept on, till only seventy were left,
And held the Spur.

'Twas thus my hero spake:
He had been left behind, and bade the men
God speed. The hour, he said, was early dawn,
Scarce six o' the clock. He closed his tired eyes   30
And then, it seemed, he opened them, and lo!
A staggering, wounded man stood in the tent
Covered from head to foot with crimson blood;
To his torn face he held a dripping cloth
And still essayed to staunch his gaping wound.

---

[8]   A place of strategic importance that was captured by the Canadians during the Battle of Passchendaele.
[9]   During World War I, "Hun" was a term for German soldiers that emphasized their supposed brutality.

My hero knew him for his tenting-mate,
A senior officer, and in command.

"We're shot to pieces, Bill!" he cried at last;
"Seventeen officers have fallen out;
There's no one left. When we'd gone o'er the top,   40
We met a galling fire from the Huns;
Machine-guns fairly bristled in the box
That crowned the height, and made it more than hard
For us to advance a paltry hundred yards,
With every foot of ground strewn thick with dead.
I left them broken, bent, but hanging on,
With two lieutenants clinging to the Spur,
And picked my way, beneath a rain of shells,
Along a road that vanished as I walked."

O ye of miserable stock! Whom he   50
Called "safety firsts," ye who took every chance
To save yourselves, once you had crossed the sea;
Better, by a hair's breadth, than slackers here!
Listen, I pray you, to what this man did
When he was left behind at Passchendaele;
No more, he said, than was his duty: yet
He did it nobly: that's enough for me.

The time was early morn, and scarcely light;
But minutes count and melt like snow in rain
When souls are being pounded out of men.   60
The breaking morning found him plunging on
Through deep morass and through a deeper mud
That caught him somewhere near or 'round the waist,
To where the old battalion held the line,
With two lieutenants clinging to the Spur.
The receding Germans yielding inch by inch,
And raining tons of missiles on our men.

With no emplacements[10] for our lurching guns
In the quaking lake of fusing mire and earth,
And nothing left to do but drag them up,   70
As best we could, through miles of oozing mud,
Our troops drove back the Huns, dented and breached
Their wall of steel, and so forever laid
In the mire the arrogance and vaunted might
That hurled their challenge at a peaceful world.

All day the battle raged, but stubborn men
Pressed on the massive "pill-box" on the height
And stormed it, smashing up the battery
That wrought such havoc in the early morn.
Then what was left of the old 58th   80
Came on, to find their wounded and their dead
Strewing the blood-soaked swamps like withered leaves
That fall before the autumn's levelling blast.

Where were the wounded? Did I ask, or did
My soldier tell me how the fallen fared?
Ere yet the height was stormed, from break of day
And through the tedious hours that make the time
We call the morning and the afternoon,
They lay unsuccoured[11] on the battle-field
Where first they fell, nor any aid received,   90
Nor dressings of their wounds, till battle's flame
Had swept beyond the Spur and passed them by,
Leaving them prone in face of victory.

So hot had been the shelling of the morn
That none might venture in the zone of fire
And live; but towards the set of sun there came

---

[10] platform for guns
[11] unattended .

Surgeons and helpers; these it was who bore
And drew as many as the fort would hold
To safety, and to rest upon the floor.

And here my soldier found them late at night,   100
After the heavy fighting of the day.
Battered and spent and seeking rest as well,
He, with his comrades, came to Bellevue Spur.
Entering the massive structure on the height
He found the sick and dying on the floor
So closely packed that one might barely pick
A single step between them as they lay;
Nor could my hero more than find a space
To stand on, after he had entered in.

What could be done? His mind flashed quick as light   110
The day was won! But this—! A sergeant's voice
Broke the swift flight of thought: the reliving force,
He said, had come at last; but what about
The wounded? They could not be left behind,
For never does the British soldier leave
His comrades on the fields, though others come
To carry on the fight when he is spent.

At this the Second in Command rose up
And spoke to him I called my hero. Would
He face the fire of the Huns again and take   120
The wounded out? go back a thousand yards
And bring the stretcher-bearers up; then back
And back again till all were safely out?

Another heart had quailed; my soldier's word
Was, "Yes, sir"; then he faced about and plunged
Into the night and down the shell-swept road
Till coming to a place below the height,
Where there were living men, he quickly swung

Stretchers and stretcher-bearers into line,
Sixty in number; then moved up again   130
'Neath heavy fire, to the pill-box on the hill.
Five trips in all. A last man, sorely hit,
Begged mercy when a loud, exploding shell
Struck on the battered trench, and all seemed lost.
Four prisoner Huns, there were, who took him out.
The wounded were evacuated; more,
Were taken to a place of safety; then
With scarcely strength to stand, my hero went
Once more to the front: he bearing in his lung
The German bullet got at Ypres, a year   140
Or more, before the attack at Passchendaele,
Gathered the men together and brought out
The constituent battalion: seventy men.

Did the wounded praise him for his heart of gold,
His fearless courage under heavy fire,
His gift for organizing and his speed?
Yes: you may take my word, they did; and more;
Called him "Priceless thing," as soldiers do;
Said he had won the coveted V.C.
And Military Cross, each to his mind;   150
For had he not with valour bravely saved
A dozen score or more of human lives,
Under terrific fire from the foe,
Drum-fire, it was, and brought them proudly back
To peace and safety, well behind the guns?

Yes! And the Second in Command had nought
But words of commendation. Warmly wrung
His hand (again, as soldiers do), and thanked
Him gravely: Said his work had been the best
Done at "the show" that day. His Colonel, too,   160
Praised him unstintingly, and so it was
My hero walked content: his work well done.

Such is the heroic story told, in part,
By him who ever honoured Duty first;
Who splendid passed, at Lens,[12] to his reward;
Who never knew retreat before the Hun,
And laid him down, in France, beloved of all
For long and gallant service in the line.

                                                    (1920)

Requiem[13]

If you would make a carven stone for me,
Grave[14] me as one low-lying in the dust
Before a soldier form, erect and full
Of pride; and say of me: "She was not meet
To bind the latchet of his shoe, and yet
He loved her; held her dear and dearer still
Before he fell; was ever proud to call
Her 'Mother'; glad to hear her voice; to catch
The low, articulate sound that named him hers."

And carve him standing in an aureole[15] light,   10
With laurel crown upon his victor's head,
And face upturned; and say: "While much he loved
This woman at his feet, she was but clay
When likened to the Cause for which he died."

                                                    (1920)

---

[12] A town in France that had particular strategic importance during the spring and late summer of 1917; Canadians staged a successful campaign at Hill 70 (sometimes called the Battle of Lens) in August 1917.
[13] Specifically, the Roman Catholic mass for the dead; generally, any song on the occasion of a burial.
[14] engrave
[15] halo

A Soldier's Grave in France

Here lies a widowed mother's only son.
O gentle winds! temper the airs of heav'n
That they blow softly where his young head rests
In friendly soil, rich-carpeted with bloom:
Scarlet and gentian blue and butter-gold,
Flecked with an English daisy here and there.
He was no dreamer, though he soundly sleeps;
Rather a man in whom the joy of life
Foamed sparkling to the brim; and when great France
Sent forth her bitter, wailing cry for help,   10
(That France which holds him here enclasped in earth)
Eastward he turned his face and crossed the seas,
Laid youth and glorious manhood in the dust,
And so stepped into immortality.

(1920)

Sunrise in France

I saw the rosy dawn stream o'er your grave
Near ruined Lens;[16] then grow to yellow gold,
And day's first glory break in th' east, to which
Your quiet face is turned. You only sleep:
There must be something, 'neath an alien soil.
Of that immortal radiance men call life,
That made you what you were: the cheeriest soul
That e'er was born. But look! The sun mounts higher,
And a dark, outstretched arm is thrown athwart
The bending poppies; a long cross steals out,   10

---

[16] A town in France that had particular strategic importance during the spring and late summer of 1917; Canadians staged a successful campaign at Hill 70 (sometimes called the Battle of Lens) in August 1917.

Black as the shadow in my aching heart;
A shade that ne'er was meant to mingle with
The sunshine on your grave: That should be pure
As beaten gold; and as cheerful as were you.

(1920)

Vimy Ridge[17]
April 9, 1917

The cross I wear? That came from Vimy Ridge.
La Folie Farm,[18] which always makes a bridge
Between my mind and the battle. The scarred wood
Was picked up by my hero, when he stood
After the fight on Vimy, and for me
Sought out the shattered fragments of a tree,
The pieces somewhat larger than the match
With which he lit his pipe. But do you catch
The blaze of the world "Lens"[19] across the arms?
That's where my soldier fell. La Folie Farm's   10

A name that burns and flames, and stands to be
Immortal. Now to the great victory
Of Vimy Ridge. The tale is scarcely new.
How to describe it from his point of view
Who only saw a section of the fight!
One section only? God! can this be right?
Nothing he spake of fearless, dying eyes
Looking to Heaven; nor of the anguished cries
Rending the air. He told his story while
I sat enthralled, as shaded word and style   20

---

[17] The location in France of one of Canada's more successful and famous battles. After months
of preparations, the battle lasted only a few days in the spring of 1917, and was celebrated by
Canadians as a crucial victory.

[18] A town in France that had particular strategic importance during the spring and late summer
of 1917; Canadians staged a successful campaign at Hill 70 (sometimes called the Battle of
Lens) in August 1917.

[19] A town in France and a strategic location during and after the Battle of Vimy Ridge.

Brought clear before my eyes what he had seen.
Nought of the horrors spake he, though I ween[20]
His eyes, before that famous height was won
Had looked on that which shamed all horrors done.

Easter Day dawned: the eve of the big push
At Vimy Ridge. My hero felt a hush
Of peace, and willed to meet his Blessed Lord
In the Bread and Wine; but he could not afford
Time for the sacred rite, for all day through
He worked, nor one short moment's leisure knew.   30
His was a preparation for the day
We rose to life; though on Vimy death held sway.
But, when the sun was set there came a call
To solemn service in the field, and all
Answered the summons of the Church parade,
Which to their work a fitting ending made.
Ah, me! Ere the morrow's sun could seek his grave
How many would be sleeping with the brave?
Our men, Canadians, who that we might live
Unfettered here, gave all that men could give!   40

The padre's voice had scarcely ceased from prayer
When distant rounds of cheering tore the air;
Wild, yet harmonious; then loud song burst forth
As if in answer to a challenge; worth
A hundred sermons to the men who stood
And waited while the approaching rhythmic flood
Of sound came nearer, and a singing throng
Of marching men came rank on rank along:

The glorious Fourth Division! Theirs to die,
Nor once to count the cost. 'Twas thus passed by   50

---

[20] believe, surmise

The assaulting forces! Thus that to them came
The honour first to make great Vimy's name,
And without warning drive the entrenchèd Hun
Like hasty scampering rats that fear the sun.
To earth. My soldier, he who later fell
At Lens, declared no words of his could tell
With what swinging gait our men passed by,
Marching, with song, to death and victory.

And once more silence reigned. Ere his turn came
He looked out o'er the lines: all was serene   60
Except for a gun's flash. Then with his men
He moved up to position and dug in,
And with his batman[21] waited till the dawn,
Watching, meanwhile, an airplane, now withdrawn,
Now sweeping forward. Then all hell broke loose!
The awful, flashing British guns that choose
To belch and vomit flame, had opened fire
On the dazed foe, forcing him to retire.

British artillery! searching every hand
Of ground. Tingling with victory and manned   70
With steadied will, under the blackened sky
My hero heard the missiles hurtling by
Charged with destruction; knew the objective won,
Though pandemonium reigned; the fight begun,
Under twelve creeping barrages they advanced,
Waiting ten minutes while above them danced
The raining shells; ten straining minutes, then
They onward drove straight at the fringe of the rain
Of fire; made the disordered foeman run,
Nor stop to staunch the gaping wound that none   80
Could stop nor staunch; that our men, pressing on,

---

[21]   an officer's personal servant

Breached to twelve thousand yards. Before the sun
Had time to stain the east, a blinding storm
Of snow was falling on the Ridge, a form
Of sleet and rain that drenched the men and left
Them chilled and cold, but pushing through the cleft
Our guns had made. The minutes sped and morn
Broke slowly over trenches scarred and torn
With shrapnel. All day long, from time to time
In gusty sequence, then in booming rhyme,   90
The artillery flashed and thundered, and the Huns
Replied: but our supporters pressed on, while tons
Of shells burst everywhere. For ten long days
The battle raged. The price was paid. (A maze
Of ghostly crosses marks the toll of lives.
You see the outstretched arms as your car dives
Into the Arras[22] road to-day. 'Tis said
The Risen Lord Himself walks 'midst the dead.)

There youth and splendid manhood bit the dust
That we might live in freedom; we who just   100
Feel a slight tremour if our finger aches.
The story of the taken trenches makes
A tale in itself. Well, are you bored? or have
You seen the advance at Vimy as my brave
Heart saw it? When he with his fearless men
Marched mile on mile through slush and mire, and then
Laid down, at Lens, the rich treasure of his life;
A full, sufficient, perfect sacrifice.

(1920)

---

[22] A French town that was the site of a series of protracted offensives, and is the location of a cemetery containing thousands of soldiers' graves.

William Wilfred Campbell

(1860–1918)

William Wilfred Campbell grew up in Wiarton, Ontario and later became a clergyman, a civil servant, and a poet—a role that brought him both admiration and derision. His lyrics about Lake Huron were widely celebrated by his contemporaries, and he achieved minor celebrity for his poem "The Mother," which was printed in "hundreds of publications in every English speaking country," and lauded by Sir Wilfrid Laurier.[1] But he also drew some contempt for his criticism of Charles G.D. Roberts and his parody of Archibald Lampman's poetry.

For Campbell, poetry had many roles. It provided opportunities to praise nature, to hold forth on topics of the day ranging from science to religion, and to convey genuine and meaningful emotion.

---

[1] Laurel Boone, notes to *William Wilfred Campbell: Selected Poetry and Essays* (Waterloo: Wilfrid Laurier University Press, 1987), 211. Laurel Boone has determined Campbell's birth date to be 1860, rather than 1858 or 1861 (as previously thought).

After all, in his eyes, emotion was the hallmark of great poetry. It was emotion that would "sweep like a baptismal wave from ocean to ocean and overpower all local, racial, and other influences" and bring a unified national feeling.[2]

Those overwhelming feelings are on full display in his war poetry. Biographer Laurel Boone points out that, although Campbell tried to enlist in the war, he was kept from the front because of his age and ill-health—but that did not quell his enthusiasm.[3] Campbell became an eager contributor to the war efforts on the home front, training soldiers and writing about the war for charitable benefit. In one of his touring lectures, Campbell makes clear that war was an opportunity to solidify Canada's connection to the British Empire and to "be more like Britain." "No man can hate war more than I do," Campbell goes on to say, "but there are many things in this world which we hate, which we have to contemplate and prepare for. The following verses may explain, better than my prose, my attitude towards this question."[4]

The Summons

Britons, along the mighty world's highway,
    Waken and throng, from mart and field and glen;
Now looms that day of wrath, the world's dread day,
    Prophesied of old by ancient men;—
        Arise! Arise!

From every corner of the teeming earth,
    Answer and gather, to her banners come;

---

[2] William Wilfred Campbell, "At the Mermaid Inn," *The Globe*, December 31, 1892: 8.

[3] Laurel Boone, introduction to *William Wilfred Campbell: Selected Poetry and Essays*, 7.

[4] William Wilfred Campbell, "Canada's Responsibility to the Empire and the Race," in *William Wilfred Campbell: Selected Poetry and Essays*, ed. Laurel Boone (Waterloo: Wilfrid Laurier University Press, 1987), 199.

Throw down the duty or the dice of mirth,
   Responsive to the ominous battle drum:
      Prepare! Prepare!   10

This is no hour for hesitating doubt,
   Self interest's greed, or base ambition's dream
The grim red wolves of earth's worst war are out
   The iron menace and the balefire's gleam
      Enlist! Enlist!

The arrogant Hun against our ancient coasts
   Would hurl his serried panoply of steel,
Across the world are heard the despot's boasts
   O'er Europe's land his awful cohorts reel
      Arise! Arise!   20

Waken, if e'er you woke to any cause,
   Now strikes your hour, to conquer or go down,
To win for freedom, justice and God's laws,
   Or sink before the cruel despot's crown
      Arise! Arise!

Go forth and battle as your fathers went,
   Who never let a great cause thunder down.
Those wardens, wide, on each far continent,
   Of Britain's ancient honor and renown.
      Go forth! Go forth!   30

Go forth and fight, nor will you strive alone;
   Earth's valiant ones will battle by your side;—
And strength of all that strength your cause shall own.
   The Lord of Hosts will in your vanguard ride;
      Toward earth's high doom.

                                   (1915)

Our Dead

Our dead, they are ours and the Empire's
   Till the last red sun doth set;—
And may God, in His terrible justice, deal with us,
   If we forget.

Till that which we sent them to die for,
   Till that dread struggle be won;
Though the traitor and idiot cry out for peace,
   There can be none.

We are either on God's side or evil's,
   We are either perjured or true;—   10
And that, which we set out to do in the first place,
   That must we do.

If we lie now unto our highest,
   Prove traitorous unto our best,
And soften the hand, which set out to conquer
   At God's behest;

If we fail in our vows in the slightest,
   Our pride to dishonour is thrall;—
For we stand to win all in this conflict,—
   Or else lose all.   20

There are many side-roads to oblivion,
   But only one straight to the dawn;—
And thrusting aside all paltering, faltering thought,
   We must push on.

Not fearing, nor doubting, nor halting,
   But iron-souled, centered as one
On the one grim work in this war-gripped world,
   Which must be done.

For our dead are ours and the Empire's,
   Till the last red sun doth set;—   30
And may God, in His terrible justice, deal with us,
   If we forget.

                                                    (1916)

The Fight Goes On

The fight goes on; though slower than men thought;
   But still it goes; and Britain works her way,
With her great-hearted allies; unsullied, unbought;
   Toward that true dawn which ushers freedom's day.

The fight goes on; but God demands of all,
   Heroic patience and heroic trust,
Never to swerve from that first bugle call,
   Which woke the hero in our patriot dust.

The fight goes on; though oft in darker hours,
   Faint hearts would compromise with freedom's foe;   10
But unto such, though traitor cowardice cowers,
   Each blooddrop of our slain ones answers, No!

In this grim strife, where Crime and Judgement meet,
   And earth's great flags for freedom's cause unfurled,
Better go under in some dread defeat,
   Than compromise with what would crush this world.

                                                    (1917)

Langemarck[5]
(*April 26–29, 1915*)

This is the ballad of Langemarck,
   A story of glory and might;
Of the vast Hun horde, and Canada's part
   In the great, grim fight.

It was April fair on the Flanders field,
   But the dreadest April then,
That ever the years, in their fateful flight,
   Had brought to this world of men.

North and east, a monster wall,
   The mighty Hun ranks lay,   10
With fort on fort, and iron-ringed trench,
   Menacing, grim and gray.

And south and west, like a serpent of fire,
   Serried the British lines,
And in between, the dying and dead,
And the stench of blood, and the trampled mud,
   On the fair, sweet Belgian vines.

And far to the eastward, harnessed and taut,
   Like a scimitar, shining and keen,
Gleaming out of that ominous gloom,   20
   Old France's hosts were seen.

When out of the grim Hun lines one night,
   There rolled a sinister smoke;—
A strange, weird cloud, like a pale, green shroud,
   And death lurked in its cloak.

---

[5] The battle described here, usually known as part of the Second Battle of Ypres, was one of the first occasions when the Germans used gas on Canadian troops.

On a fiend-like wind it curled along
    Over the brave French ranks,
Like a monster tree its vapors spread,
    In hideous, burning banks
Of poisonous fumes that scorched the night   30
    With their sulphurous demon danks.[6]

And men went mad with horror, and fled
    From that terrible strangling death,
That seemed to sear both body and soul
    With its baleful, flaming breath.

Till even the little dark men of the south,
    Who feared neither God nor man,
Those fierce, wild fighters of Afric's steppes,
    Broke their battalions and ran—

Ran as they never had run before,   40
    Gasping, and fainting for breath;
For they knew 'twas no human foe that slew;
    And that hideous smoke meant death.

Then red in the reek of that evil cloud,
    The Hun swept over the plain;
And the murderer's dirk[7] did its monster work,
    Mid the scythe-like shrapnel rain.

Till it seemed that at last, the brute Hun hordes,
    Had broken that wall of steel;
And that soon, through this breach in the freeman's dyke,   50
    Their trampling hosts would wheel;—

---

[6] humidity, wetness, water
[7] dagger

And sweep to the south in ravaging might,
    And Europe's peoples again,
Be trodden under the tyrant's heel,
    Like herds, in the Teuton[8] pen.

But in the line on the British right,
    There massed a corps amain,
Of men who hailed from a far west land
    Of mountain and forest and plain;

Men new to war and its dreadest deeds,   60
    But noble and staunch and true;
Men of the open, East and West,
    Brew of old Britain's brew.

These were the men out there that night,
    When Hell loomed close ahead;
Who saw that pitiful, hideous rout,
    And breathed those gasses dread;
While some went under and some went mad;
    But never a man there fled.

For the word was "Canada," theirs to fight,   70
    And keep on fighting still—
Britain said, "Fight," and fight they would,
    Though the Devil himself in sulphurous mood,
Come over that hideous hill.

Yea, stubborn, they stood, that hero band,
    Where no soul hoped to live;
For five, 'gainst eighty thousand men,
    Were hopeless odds to give.

---

[8] German

Yea, fought they on! 'Twas Friday eve,
　　When that demon gas drove down;　　　　　　　　　80
'Twas Saturday eve that saw them still
　　Grimly holding their own;

Sunday, Monday, saw them yet,
　　A steady lessening band,
With "no surrender" in their hearts,
　　But the dream of a far-off land,

Where mother and sister and love would weep
　　For the hushed heart lying still;—
But never a thought but to do their part,
　　And work the Empire's will.　　　　　　　　　　　90

Ringed round, hemmed in, and back to back,
　　They fought there under the dark,
And won for Empire, God and Right,
　　At grim, red Langemarck.

Wonderful battles have shaken this world,
　　Since Dawn-God overthrew Dis;[9]
Wonderful struggles of right against wrong,
Sung in the rhymes of the world's great song,
　　But never a greater than this.

Bannockburn, Inkerman, Balaclava,　　　　　　　　100
　　Marathon's god-like stand;[10]
But never a more heroic deed,
And never a greater warrior breed,
　　In any warman's land.

---

[9]　Roman god of the underworld
[10]　Names of battles in earlier wars where one side was outnumbered yet succeeded.

This is the ballad of Langemarck,
    A story of glory and might;
Of the vast Hun horde, and Canada's part
    In the great, grim fight.

(1917)

Helena Coleman
(1860–1953)

Born in Newcastle, Ontario to a Methodist preacher and his wife, Helena Coleman was, for a number of years, regarded as a brilliant musician and frequent traveller—but not a writer. By the time her first collection of poetry, *Songs and Sonnets*, appeared in 1906, she was already a well-published author, although few people knew it. Coleman had been writing for years under nearly a dozen pseudonyms and had published both prose and poetry in some of North America's most popular magazines. Her work's appearance in the popular press might have led to eager dismissal by highbrow critics, had it not been of such high quality. Writing in *Canadian Magazine*, Professor W.T. Allison assured readers that Coleman's poetry was surely different from other "latter day magazine versifiers." She might address the common topics of nature and beauty, but there is also, he wrote, "in her bracing pages … gentle pessimism [and] we discover over and over again that she too is acquainted with the doubt and restless intellectual questioning of our day in matters of faith."[1]

During the war, Coleman published *Marching Men: War Verses* (1917). Most reviews praised the collection, celebrating its moments of patriotic fervour. But the review that appeared in the University of Toronto's *The Rebel Magazine* struck a slightly different note and recognized the poetry's ambivalence, interest in loss, pain, sacrifice, and enthusiasm. *Marching Men*, said *The Rebel*'s critic, is the sort of "true poetry [that] begins to issue forth" during a crisis, "like the blood of the grapes, crushed in the winepress of affliction."[2] Though she would continue to write after the war, *Marching Men* was Coleman's last collection of poetry.

Challenge

Soldier, by thy blade to-night
Keen and hungry, ruthless, bright;
Be thy strong right arm unsparing,
Swift to do thy spirit's daring;
Let the God within thee waken,
Lead thee onward to thy height,
Let no citadel be taken
In thy hidden self to-night,
But with soul resolved, unshaken,
Trust the larger faith and fight!   10

Heir art thou of all the past;
Let its judgments bind thee fast.
Let the ages speak again
Through the hearts of living men;

[1] W.T. Allison, "A New Voice in Canadian Literature," *Canadian Magazine*, February 1907, 405–406.
[2] "Literary Drummer," a review of *Marching Men* by Helena Coleman, *The Rebel*, December 1917, 124.

Never was such passion laid
On our shrinking flesh as now
Never such a price was paid
For the fealty³ men avow;
Solider, this my prayer to-night,
That thy fathers serve thee well,   20
That their blood and valor tell,
And thy living sword a-light
Charge the very gates of Hell—
For the God of ages fight!

Soldier, if in this night's reaping
Thou be of the harvest found,
Should death take thee into keeping,
Sharer of the soulless ground,
Yet stand fast with sword uplifted,
Wheat from chaff is surely sifted;   30
Though thou leave all earth behind thee
Never fear but love will find thee;
Lies the issue on the altar,
Ours to dare and never falter.

Soldier, far from thee I stand,
Yet I take thee by the hand,
Doff this woman's robe of weakness,
This inheritance of meekness,
Bid thee harden to the strife,
In the hour supreme of life,   40
Praying with my heart aflame
As I face the stars to-night;
Worthy be thou of thy name,
Deadly be thy sword and bright,—
Heaven send thee will to fight!

(1917)

---

³ loyalty

Convocation Hall
May 18th, 1917

They rose,
The honored and the grave,
The reverend, the grey,
While one read out the names of those
Who, gallant, young and brave,
Upon the field of battle gave
Their ardent lives away.

They rose to honor Youth—
What honor could they give?
What tribute shall we lay   10
Who still in safety live?
Before the shrine of those who pay
The price of honor and of truth
Giving their lives away?

They rose in reverence, yea;
But those who lie
Far on the Flanders field to-day
Had not an answering word to say;
Their silence thundered their reply—
They gave their lives away!   20

(1917)

The Day He Went

The morning dawned both bright and clear,
   That unforgotten day he went,
The hills were blue and very near
   As if for their encouragement.

The rose that was her special care,
    Had come to color over night,
And lifted to the radiant air
    A bud half-blown—a lovely sight.

He paused a moment by its side,
    Their mingling glances on it fell,   10
Then his roamed where the hills divide,
    Taking of them a mute farewell.

He swept the horizon half around,
    Standing erect with kindling[4] eye
That rested where the slope pine-crowned
    Went climbing up to meet the sky.

And then to her—with one deep look
    That knit her spirit to his own,
Courage and strength of him she took,
    And heart to face the road alone.   20

No word was said; the years behind
    Held no regret; and each to each
Gave pledge of what their souls divined
    Better in silence than in speech.

                                                    (1917)

Marching Men

Flaring bugle, throbbing drum,
Onward, onward hear them come,
Like a tide along the street
Swells the sound of martial feet;

---

4   burning or combustible

On the breeze their colors streaming,
In the sun their rifles gleaming,
Pride of country, pride of race,
Glowing in each ruddy face—
   Marching men, marching men,
Leaping pulses keep you pace.   10

Measured, rhythmic, thousands strong,
Sounds their tread the whole night long,
Beating over heart and brain,
Over hopes that bloomed in vain,
Like the roll of distant thunder,
That would tear a world asunder,
All the nation's hope and pride
Surging in the tireless tide—
   Marching men, marching men,
Love goes praying by your side.   20

Deep the pathways they have worn
Over women's hearts forlorn,
Over lives grown thin and failing,
Where the stars of hope are paling:
Children's arms they must unbind,
Love and laugher leave behind,
Turn them from the beckoning morrow,
And the praying hands of sorrow,
Turn them to a place of dread
Where the skies burn darkly red,—   30
   Marching men, marching men,
Grief shall follow in your tread.

From the silver coasts outlying,
Where the pallid ships are plying,
Sweeping in from East and West,
Over crag and mountain crest,
Up from desert, grove and glen,

Still there come those hosts of men;
In their hands the sword aflame,
On their lips an ancient name,   40
Cleaving hearts and lives asunder,
Trampling thrones and empires under;
Temples lately love forsaken
They have entered and retaken,
Earth itself their tread has shaken—
    Marching men, marching men
Sleeping gods your shouts awaken!

                                  (1917)

Oh, Not When April Wakes the Daffodils

Oh, not when April wakes the daffodils,
    And bob-o-links[5] o'er misty meadows ring
Their fluted bells, and orchards fleeced with Spring;
Go climbing up to crown the radiant hills;
Not when the budding balm-o'-gilead[6] spills
    Its spices on the air, and lilacs bring
    Old dreams to mind, and every living thing
The brimming cup with fresh enchantment fills.

Oh, bring not then the dread report of death,—
    Of eyes to loveliness forever sealed,   10
Of youth that perished as a passing breath,
Of hearts laid waste and agonies untold,
    When here in every sweet Canadian field
Are heaped such treasuries of green and gold!

                                  (1917)

---

[5] small songbirds
[6] Flowering plant or tree that is said to have healing properties; see also Jeremiah 8:22.

Pro Patria Mortui[7]

Say not they died for us;
Say, rather, with their hearts aflame,
They faced the sceptered shame,
Not counting for themselves the cost,
Well knowing else, a world were lost.
For this they came;
For this they died;
For this their death is justified.

Say not they die;
Say, rather, with youth's larger trust,   10
Into the featureless, far unknown,
Challenging love's integrity,
They spring from earth's recoiling dust.
Could greater be?
Can love disown?
Can truth be overthrown?

Say not for us they died;
They touched that dimly-visioned height
The ever-enlarging soul of man
Has yet to climb; their feet outran   20
The world's slow gait; their spirits range
In circling flight
The unconjectured fields of light.
For this they suffered change;
For this they died;
For this their death is justified.

(1917)

---

[7] "They died for their country" (Latin).

The Recruit

Through all the anguish of these days,
    The haunting horror and the woe,
One thought can set my heart ablaze
    My memory aglow.

It is his look just as he turned
    After the last good-byes were said,
A look as though for him there burned
    Some beacon-light ahead.

As though beyond the farthest thought
    Of this dark world's horizon rim,   10
Some star of faith by us uncaught
    Swung into range for him.

As though his spirit, winged, had flown
    Past stormy seas on some far quest,
And like a bird had found its own
    Hid in a quiet nest.

                                        (1917)

'Tis Not the Will That's Wanted

Would God that mine were better luck
    Than falls to the lot of woman,
In these great days with the world ablaze
    And Britain's face to the foeman;
In these great days when the hour has struck
Calling for every ounce of pluck—
God help me not to curse my luck
    That I was born a woman!

Oh, for the stinging lash of the spray,
   Green waves and wild commotion   10
The lowering fogs where grim sea-dots
   Stalk ever the Northern ocean;
Watching by night, watching by day,
Ribbons of smoke in the offing grey,
Holding the Hun and his hordes at bay
     Far in the wild North ocean!

Oh, for the airman's sinuous flight,
   The great wings climbing, curving,
To desperate deeds as earth recedes
   One's tightened pulses nerving,   20
Over the hostile camps at night,
Where red eyes gleam through the murky light,
A blow to strike for freedom's right
     The God of freedom serving!

Or out on the tortured fields of France
   Where hellish deeds are flaunted,
With face to the Rhine on the firing line
   To stand with a heart undaunted;
'Mid screaming shell and shrapnel dance
Unmoved by outer circumstance,   30
To serve one's turn and take one's chance—
     'Tis not the will that's wanted!

                    (1917)

When First He Put the Khaki On

When first he put the khaki on
   He tried with careful art
To seem blasé and casual
   And play the proper part,

But it was plain as plain could be
    He was a child at heart.

Although he talked in knowing terms
    Of what "the boys" had done,
Likewise of ammunition tests,
    And how to load a gun,   10
And bragged that in his stocking feet
    He stood full six foot, one.

Yet all the while the child looked out
    With mild appealing eyes,
Unconscious he was visible
    Beneath the man's disguise,
Nor dreaming what the look evoked
    In hearts grown mother-wise.

How could he know the sudden pang,
    The stir of swift alarms,   20
The yearning prayer that innocence
    Be kept from all that harms,
The inner reach of tenderness,
    And cradling of soft arms?

                                                    (1917)

Charles G.D. Roberts
(1860–1943)

Charles G.D. Roberts rose to prominence as the lead figure of the Confederation Group of Poets. After a childhood in New Brunswick, he left for Toronto and then moved on to New York, travelled around Europe, and eventually returned to Canada as a celebrated and prolific author of nature poems and animal stories. A landmark of Canadian literature, Roberts's *Orion, and Other Poems* (1880) signalled the beginning of a new kind of poetry—a poetry marked by its Romantic ironies, natural landscapes, occasional abstractions, and introspective personae.

Roberts was undoubtedly enthusiastic for the war. For him, the Great War was a chance to prove his own personal worth and defend the honour of the Empire. He wrote to his son Douglas on 4 October 1914, "I am coming to the feeling that it would be actual relief and blessed comfort to lie in the trench with my cheek to the rifle, & just give oneself, give oneself utterly, for all that we stand for in this war."[1]

Despite his longing for the front, Roberts spent a good deal of time in a support role, first breaking horses, then training soldiers. Only by lying about his age did he move closer to the action (by way of a commission to the British forces), but ended up working in the Canadian War Records Office alongside Sir Max Aitken. Roberts was responsible for writing the third volume of the official *Canada in Flanders* (1918), which was praised by most but criticized by Arthur Currie for its occasional errors and inaccuracies.

The poems collected here were written at different times during the war and offer two very different perspectives. Laurel Boone reasonably concludes that "Cambrai and Marne" was the poem included in the letter to his daughter, Edith, in 1914.[2] According to Desmond Pacey, "Going Over" was written in the last year of the war.[3]

Cambrai and Marne[4]

Before our trenches at Cambrai
We saw their columns cringe away.
We saw their masses melt and reel
Before our line of leaping steel.
A handful to their storming hordes

We scourged them with the scourge of swords,
And still, the more we slew, the more
Came up for every slain a score.
Between the hedges and the town
Their cursing squadrons we rode down.   10

---

[1]   Charles G.D. Roberts to Douglas Roberts, 4 October 1914, in *The Collected Letters of Sir Charles G.D. Roberts*, ed. Laurel Boone (Fredericton: Goose Lane Editions, 1989), 301.
[2]   Boone, *Collected Letters*, 300.
[3]   Desmond Pacey, *The Collected Poems of Sir Charles G.D. Roberts* (Wolfville, NS: Wombat Press, 1985), 533. Pacey also notes that in later editions, the poem was subtitled "The Somme, 1917."
[4]   Cambrai, a town in France, was taken by the Germans in August 1914. The Battle of Marne occurred in September 1914 and slowed the German progress through France.

To stay them we outpoured our blood
Between the beetfields and the wood.
In that red hell of shrieking shell
Unfaltering our gunners fell.
They fell, or ere that day was done,

Beside the last unshattered gun.
But still we held them, like a wall
On which the breakers vainly fall—
Till came the word, and we obeyed,
Reluctant, bleeding, undismayed.   20

Our feet, astonished, learned retreat,
Our souls rejected still defeat.
Unbroken still, a lion at bay,
We drew back grimly from Cambrai.
In blood and sweat, with slaughter spent,

They thought us beaten as we went;
Till suddenly we turned and smote
The shout of triumph in their throat.
At last, at last we turned and stood—
And Marne's fair water ran with blood.   30

We stood by trench and steel and gun,
For now the indignant flight was done.
We ploughed their shaken ranks with fire.
We trod their masses into mire.
Our sabres drove through their retreat,

As drives the whirlwind through young wheat.
At last, at last we flung them back
Along their drenched and smoking track.
We hurled them back, in blood and flame,
The reeking ways by which they came.   40

By cumbered road and desperate ford,
How fled their shamed and harassed horde!
Shout, Sons of Freemen, for the day
When Marne so well avenged Cambrai!

(1919)

Going Over

A girl's voice in the night troubled my heart
Across the roar of the guns, the crash of the shells,
Low and soft as a sigh, clearly I heard it.

Where was the broken parapet, crumbling about me?
Where my shadowy comrades, crouching expectant?
A girl's voice in the dark troubled my heart.

A dream was the ooze of the trench, the wet clay slipping.
A dream the sudden out-flare of the wide-flung Verys.[5]
I saw but a garden of lilacs, a-flower in the dusk.

What was the sergeant saying?—I passed it along.—   10
Did *I* pass it along? I was breathing the breath of the lilacs.
For a girl's voice in the night troubled my heart.

Over! How the mud sucks! Vomits red the barrage.
But I am far off in the hush of a garden of lilacs.
For a girl's voice in the night troubled my heart.
Tender and soft as a sigh, clearly I heard it.

(1919)

---

[5] flares

Frederick George Scott
(1861–1944)

Frederick George Scott was born in Montreal and was an active, though minor, member of the Confederation Group of Poets. An ordained member of the clergy and a prolific writer (of prose, poetry, and drama), Scott enjoyed considerable attention, both domestic and international, especially for his verse. Charles G.D. Roberts, for instance, declared that Scott's poem "Samson" (1894) was "[o]ne of the best poems we Canadians have produced";[1] his "Requiescant" was published in London's *The Times* in 1915.

Scott joined the war immediately, saw routine action at the front for almost four years, and stayed in Europe well after the Armistice was declared. From the beginning, his motivation was persistent and religious. If a chaplain ran away from battle, he wrote, "about six hundred men would say at once, 'We have no use for religion.'"[2]

[1] Charles G.D. Roberts to Frederick George Scott, 4 February 1893, in Boone, *Collected Letters*, 168.
[2] Scott, *Great War*, 15.

So, he went to war to defend his country and to prove the value of his vocation. In 1916 Scott published *In the Battle Silences*, a surprisingly uniform collection of fervently patriotic panegyrics and consoling elegies. In 1924 he published a memoir, *The Great War As I Saw It*, which offers a decidedly different interpretation of the war. As M. Jeanne Yardley points out, it is an unbalanced mix of battle romance, cynicism, heroism, and horror.[3] Scott lost two sons in the war; his third, F.R. Scott, went on to become one of Canada's first fully-fledged modernist writers.

A Canadian

The glad and brave young heart
   Had come across the sea,
He longed to play his part
   In crushing tyranny.

The mountains and the plains
   Of his beloved land
Were wine within his veins
   And gave an iron hand.

He scorned the thought of fear,
   He murmured not at pain,   10
The call of God was clear,
   The path of duty plain.

Beneath the shower of lead
   Of poison and of fire,
He charged and fought and bled
   Ablaze with one desire.

---

[3] M. Jeanne Yardely, "'The Bitterness and Greatness': Reading F.G. Scott's War," *Studies in Canadian Literature* 16, no. 1 (1991).

O Canada, with pride
   Look up and greet the morn,
Since of thy wounded side
   Such breed of men is born.   20

VLAMERTINGHE, NEAR YPRES.
   27 April 1915[4]

                             (1916)

A Grave in Flanders

All night the tall trees over-head
   Are whispering to the stars;
Their roots are wrapped about the dead
   And hide the hideous scars.

The tide of war goes rolling by,
   The legions sweep along;
And daily in the summer sky
   The birds will sing their song.

No place is this for human tears,
   The time for tears is done;   10
Transfigured in these awful years,
   The two worlds blend in one.

This boy had visions while in life
   Of stars on distant skies;
So death came in the midst of strife
   A sudden, glad surprise.

He found the songs for which he yearned,
   Hopes that had mocked desire;

---

[4] The place and date suggest this poem was written on the occasion of the Second Battle of Ypres in late April 1915.

His heart is resting now which burned
    With such consuming fire.   20

So down the ringing road we pass,
    And leave him where he fell,
The guardian trees, the waving grass,
    The birds will love him well.

                           (1916)

Requiescant[5]

In lonely watches night by night
Great visions burst upon my sight,
For down the stretches of the sky
The hosts of dead go marching by.

Strange ghostly banners o'er them float,
Strange bugles sound an awful note,
And all their faces and their eyes
Are lit with starlight from the skies.

The anguish and the pain have passed
And peace hath come to them at last,   10
But in the stern looks linger still
The iron purpose and the will.

Dear Christ, who reign'st above the flood
Of human tears and human blood,
A weary road these men have trod,
O house them in the home of God.

    IN A FIELD NEAR YPRES.
      April 1915

                           (1916)

---

[5]   "They lie" (Latin).

Duncan Campbell Scott

(1862–1947)

Few poets in Canadian literature are as polarizing as Duncan Campbell Scott. For some, his poetry is an extension of (and over-shadowed by) his work at the Department of Indian Affairs and its policies of assimilation. For others, such as critic Leslie Ritchie, Scott is an important member of Canada's Confederation Group of Poets and "a cultural icon," someone who lives up to his assessment of his status as "the austere artist, the poet's poet."[1]

Scott was born in Ottawa and, at a young age, entered into the civil service, working his way up the ranks of the Department of Indian Affairs. Inspired by fellow poet and civil servant Archibald Lampman, Scott began to write about the backwoods of Ontario and Quebec and, later, the native people he and his department had been asked to govern.

---

[1]   Leslie Ritchie, introduction to *Addresses, Essays, Reviews*, by Duncan Campbell Scott (London: Canadian Poetry Press, 2000), xii–xiii.

Scott's work in the Department of Indian Affairs has justifiably directed scholarly attention to his poems about aboriginal people, but he did write about other subjects, including Rupert Brooke's life and poetry and World War I. Brooke stayed at Scott's Ottawa home for a week before the war broke out, and the effect of that meeting was lasting. As late as 1922, in his essay "Poetry and Progress," Scott recalled fondly his time spent with Brooke and the "intensity of feeling" in those "incomparable sonnets of his" and their indisputable "genius."[2] The ideas and sentiments in Brooke's sonnets appear here in Scott's war poetry, alongside other concerns about the roles of art, women, and nature.

Somewhere in France

The storm was done
And fragments of the sun
Fell on the great Cathedral front
Of saints and heroes,
And touched a woman's form
Vanishing through the porch,
She pushed the leathern door
And saw the great rose-window like a torch
Colour the milliard ghosts of the dead incense.
She paused at the *bénitier*[3]   10
And trembled down the aisle.
She thought to make a prayer,
She knelt but could not pray—
A month on yesterday
Her lover had been killed at Verdun.

*   *   *

---

[2]   Duncan Campbell Scott, "Poetry and Progress," *Canadian Magazine*, January 1923, 191–92.
[3]   vessel for holy water

Deep grief dawns slowly
And the light was on her soul.

*   *   *

She thought on God and called on Christ,
And fainted in her woe.
And lo!   20
As she leant against the pillar,
Pale like a saint—stiller
Than death—from out the stone
Thrilled a warm tone,
As if an Angel spoke:

*   *   *

Thou art not here alone,
Thy sorrow woke
One who once loved as thou,
Long, long ago.
Noble he was—and he stooped low,   30
His princely people said,
To crown me.
Him they banished oversea
To kill his love;
They could not—this have I for proof,
They killed me here instead,
They walled me up at night within the stone
When this church was abuilding—
A narrow niche—and I was all alone.
It did not take me long to die,   40
And now my little dust has enough room.
But love can never die,
And when I felt my heart cry out in thine
I rose after three hundred years

To kiss your tears,
And tell you that our little wells of love
Have springs in the great deeps thereof.
And this I know in mine own soul,
And by the blessed rood,[4]
There is a solitude   50
Beyond his death and thine
Where time shall have no hours,
Where you shall be together.
Till then above mischance
Thy soul is guarded in the soul of France.

*   *   *

And then the lovely shape within the stone
Fell into silence, and a little dust
Fell in the silence.

*   *   *

But she who was so strangely comforted,
Left the dim shrine,   60
And pushed the leathern door,
And stood upon the threshold in the shine
Struck from a thousand banners in the sky,
Where a great tempest-sunset marching by
Deployed before the portal
As all the flags of France were beating there
In the flushed air
Triumphant and immortal.

(1917)

---

[4]   sculpture or painting of Jesus on the cross

To a Canadian Aviator Who Died for His Country in France

Tossed like a falcon from the hunter's wrist,
A sweeping plunge, a sudden shattering noise,
And thou hast dared, with a long spiral twist,
The elastic stairway to the rising sun.
Peril below thee, and above, peril
Within thy car; but peril cannot daunt
Thy peerless heart: gathering wing and poise,
Thy plane transfigured, and thy motor-chant
Subdued to a whisper—then a silence,—
And thou art but a disembodied venture   10
In the void.

But Death, who has learned to fly,
Still matchless when his work is to be done,
Met thee between the armies and the sun;
Thy speck of shadow faltered in the sky;
Then thy dead engine and thy broken wings
Drooped through the arc and passed in fire,
A wreath of smoke—a breathless exhalation.
But ere that came a vision sealed thine eyes,
Lulling thy senses with oblivion;   20
And from its sliding station in the skies
Thy dauntless soul upward in circles soared
To the sublime and purest radiance whence it sprang.

In all their eyries,[5] eagles shall mourn thy fate,
And leaving on the lonely crags and scaurs[6]
Their unprotected young, shall congregate
High in the tenuous heaven and anger the sun

---

[5]   nests
[6]   cliffs

With screams, and with a wild audacity
Dare all the battle danger of thy flight;
Till weary with combat one shall desert the light,   30
Fall like a bolt of thunder and check his fall
On the high ledge, smoky with mist and cloud,
Where his neglected eaglets shriek aloud,
And drawing the film across his sovereign sight
Shall dream of thy swift soul immortal
Mounting in circles, faithful beyond death.

                                                    (1917)

To a Canadian Lad Killed in the War

O Noble youth that held our honour in keeping,
And bore it sacred through the battle flame,
How shall we give full measure of acclaim
To thy sharp labour, thy immortal reaping?
For though we sowed with doubtful hands, half sleeping,
Thou in thy vivid pride hast reaped a nation,
And brought it in with shouts and exultation,
With drums and trumpets, with flags flashing and leaping.

                    *   *   *

Let us bring pungent wreaths of balsam, and tender
Tendrils of wild-flowers, lovelier for thy daring,   10
And deck a sylvan shrine, where the maple parts
The moonlight, with lilac bloom, and the splendour
Of suns unwearied; all unwithered wearing
Thy valour stainless in our heart of hearts.

                                                    (1917)

To the Canadian Mothers

Why mourn thy dead, that are the world's possession?
These, our Immortals—Shall we give them up
To the complaint of private loss and dole?
Nay—mourn for them, if mourn thou must,—
Grief is thy private treasure;
Thy soul alone can count its weight or measure.
But we who know they saved the world
Think of them joined to that unwithering throng,
Who in the long dread strife
Have thought and fought for Liberty: 10
When she was but a faint pulsation in the mind,
The faintest rootlet of a growing thought,
They nourished her with tears
And gave their dreams to add depth to her foliage;
And when the enemy ravaged her bright blossoms,
Drenched her with their rich blood
To prove she lived and was the ever-living.
These are the true Immortals,
The deathless ones that saved the world.

                    *   *   *

Nay, weep, if weep thou must   20
And think upon thy lad, onetime in trust
To fortune; of his gallant golden head
And all the wayward sanctities of childhood;
Of how he crowned thy life with confidences;
Of the odour of his body, lulled with sleep,
Confusing thy dim prayers for some best future
With the sheer love that is the deepest:
False fortune has destroyed her hostages!
Old joys are bitter, bitter as very death!
Let break thy heart and so be comforted.   30

                    *   *   *

Be comforted, for we have claimed the child
And taken him to be with light and glory;
Not as we knew him in his earthly days
The lovely one, the virtuous, the dauntless,—
Or one who was a boaster, thick with faults
Perchance,—but as the index of the time
The stay and nurture of the world's best hope
The peerless seed of valour and victory.

*   *   *

Here in a realm beyond the fading world,
We garner them and hold them in abeyance   40
Ere we deliver them to light and silence—
The vestiges of battle fallen away—
Fragments of storm parting about the moon,—
Here in the dim rock-chambers, garlanded
With frail sea-roses perfumed by the sea
That murmurs of renown, and murmuring,
Scatters the cool light won by the ripple
From the stormless moon, cloistered with memory,
Whose dim caves front the immortal vistas
Plangent[7] with renown, here they await   50
The light, the glory and the ultimate rest.

*   *   *

Be comforted,—nay sob, if sob thou must,
Cover thy face and dim thy hair with dust,
And we who know they live
Gather thy dead in triumph—
Exalted from the caves of memory

---

[7] loud and reverberating

Purified from the least assoil of time,—
And lay them with all that is most living,
In light transcendent,
In the ageless aisles of silence,   60
With the Immortals that have saved the world.

                                                        (1917)

John Daniel Logan
(1869–1929)

Logan was nearly fifty when he enlisted. He already had a long and varied career as a student (studying at Harvard), scholar (delivering some of the first lectures on Canadian literature), music critic (for a Toronto newspaper), and businessman (in New York and Chicago); but he would not be deterred. After serving as a Sergeant in the 85th Battalion (from his home province of Nova Scotia), Logan returned to his scholarly work and wrote with Donald French one of Canada's first literary histories, *Highways of Canadian Literature* (1924). There he would exalt the country's war poetry for the ways in which it is "inspirational and commemorative .... *Truth, beauty and the splendour of ideas*—these are the three supreme excellences of the Canadian poetry written by soldier-poets in active service on the fighting field, and by the professional or amateur non-combatant poets at home, during the war."[1]

---

[1] Donald French and John Daniel Logan, *Highways of Canadian Literature* (Toronto: McClelland & Stewart, 1924), 344–45.

Few Canadians wrote as frequently, passionately, and thoughtfully about the war as Logan. The ideas in his essays might seem conservative or Romantic; but there is no denying their remarkable intensity. Almost all of his poems are traditional elegies (in the way that Jahan Ramazani defines the genre)[2] and dramatize a concentrated, and usually successful, search for comfort or consolation in the face of devastating circumstances. Colonel W.E. Thompson of Halifax had this to say about Logan's poetry: "The War inspired the mind of the author with fresh thoughts and led him, through the close touch it gave him with men of all nations engaged in the intensely practical affairs of fighting, to a 'larger life of holier aims.'"[3]

Renouncement[4]
A Soldier's Farewell to His Beloved on His Going to War

Kiss me good-bye!—
    And think not, dear, I love thee less
    In that I haste from thy soft charms
    At War's reverberant alarms.
I am in bond to other faithfulness:
    My country calls me—I must go
    To foil my country's direst foe
    On far-off fields incarnadin'd.[5]
    But thy too tender love is blind
    With fear and cannot see   10
If that I give myself, I also, dear, give thee.

---

[2] Jahan Ramazani, *Poetry of Mourning* (Chicago: University of Chicago Press, 1994).

[3] W.E. Thompson, foreword to *The New Apocalypse and Other Poems of Days and Deeds in France*, by John Daniel Logan (Halifax: T.C. Allen, 1919), ix.

[4] In Logan's notes on the poem, he says his inspiration was Richard Lovelace's lines, "I could not love thee, dear, so much / Loed I not honor more" from "To Lucasta, Going to the Warres" (c. 1640).

[5] dyed a flesh or blood-red colour

Kiss me goodbye!—
    And let thine eyes be eloquent
    Of constant love while I am gone;
    And this will be my benison[6]
    Midst scenes where death is imminent.
Nay, dear, give me your lips—and have no dread.
    But should I fall think me not dead:
    Although I yield my mortal breath,
    We'll be inseparable in death.   20
    For this must ever be—
If that I give myself, I also, dear, give thee.

                                                  (1916)

Timor Mortis[7]
Written in Prospect of Going to the European Battle-Front

    "For he to-day that sheds his blood with me
    Shall be my brother.........
    And gentlemen in England now abed
    Shall think themselves accursed they were not here."
        Shakespeare, *King Henry V*—Act IV, sc. 3 (King's speech prior
        to the battle of Agincourt).

I wend my ways with one dire dread
Now daily in my heart:
The fear of death obsesses me—
The fear that I may pass
Too soon for my desiring eyes to see

---

6 blessing
7 "Fear of death" (Latin); a phrase found in a Roman Catholic prayer cycle for the dead ("The Office of the Dead") and in medieval poetry; the full phrase usually is, "Timor mortis conturbat me" which translates to "The fear of death disturbs me." Logan writes, "The philosophy of the poem is, of course, that there comes to the finite individual a time when his person and deeds *can* have significance for the Infinite, and that to miss that great opportunity, through the accident of death is to have lived and died in vain—possibly, too, in dishonor."

The English camps, and for my feet to tread
The English green-sward grass;
That I who've heard my God's, my King's, my Country's claims
And, though belated, have at length begun
A larger life of holier aims   10
Than was my wont, may suddenly depart
This shattered world to utter oblivion,
Ere I, in Christian chivalry,
With brave, devoted comrades dauntlessly have stood face to the foe
On Flanders' fatal fields and struck a single blow
For man's dear brotherhood and worldwide liberty,
Or ere, upon the blood-steeped slopes
Of France, I've met—mine eyes affront, my soul quite undismayed—
The Hunnish cannons' fearful fusillade[8]
Or done my share to still the Hunnish hopes,   20
And thus to leave secure, ev'n if by my poor martyrdom,
A happier heritage to generations yet to come.

Dear God, oh, privilege me the fullest bloom
Of vital-strength, that I may pay the price
For my too selfish, easeful days; spare me to live
That I, if it should be Thy will, may sacrifice
The meagre all I now can give,
And, falling, like obscurely laid within a nameless tomb.
Perchance, round where mine unknown grave may be,
Unshaded by Canadian maples, unsung by winds from my Acadian sea, 30
I shall in spirit-state revisit foreign slope or plain
On which I fell, and there aloft descry
The Flag of England still flaunting victory to the sky,
'Neath where the hellish holocaust once swept amain,[9]
And I shall know I died not in dishonour nor in vain,

---

[8] firing of many guns simultaneously
[9] Cf. Rupert Brooke's sonnet "The Soldier": "If I should die, think only this of me: / That there's some corner of a foreign field / That is for ever England. There shall be / In that rich earth

But that I may, at home, in peace, untried, yield up my breath—
This is my direst dread, my fear, of thee, O Death!

(1916)

Farewell to France

Now have my glorious days in France at length
Run their adventurous course. The wonted strength
Of my prime years remains no longer mine,
Worn out by moiling[10] months in camp and line.
I yield to Time's concealed, relentless raids,
Insidious and silent enfilades,[11]
And cease my proud support of human laws
Against the Hun and his Hadean[12] cause.

Yet am I recompensed with ministries
Above all price—evangel[13] memories   10
Of days and nights that cannot lose their thrall,
And scenes suffused with beauty magical,
And love triumphant and the spectacle
Of sacrificial deeds no tongue can tell,—
All that enthrones the Spirit of Romance,
The glamor and the glory that are France.

O land of beauty, faith and valiant deed,
Thou'rt dear as mine own land, since sactuaried
'Neath thy green mold beloved comrades lie:
Their dust and holy sacrifices sanctify   20
Thy hills and vales. There shall they sweetly rest,

---

[10] wallowing in mud; working hard or toiling
[11] a kind of sweeping gunfire
[12] of or belonging to Hades, Greek god of the dead
[13] Specifically, good news of the redemption of the world by the sacrifice of Jesus; generally, any good news.

Clasped close, O France, to thy soft, throbbing breast.[14]
Farewell, but oft in spirit I'll come back
And dwell with them in my heart's bivouac.[15]

(1919)

The Immortal Bonds

There is a holy, happy fellowship
None but the veteran soldier knows—
A secret fellowship of friends who slip,
Unseen, into his chambered recess of repose:
Soon as the tawnied dusk of twilight dies,
They come, and fill their shadowy visitings
With low-voiced laughter; and, with shining spectral eyes,
Recount, in ghostly whisperings,
How they went forth to battle, and never recked[16] at all the cost,
Though some had fallen at Vimy and some at Passchendaele[17] were lost.   10
Or, when on people street he seems uncomraded,
They crowd to him, fall in, and, tramp, with rhythmic tread,
The City ways. Along with him they swiftly swing,
And only he is conscious of their glad companioning.

Oh, Comrades of mine who nobly fought and who were slain,
Death cannot cleave us, though I alone remain.
Still are you near me, through dark day and through red night—
Still go we together, triumphing, down to the fight.

There is a poignant, pining loneliness
None but the veteran soldier knows—   20

---

[14] Cf. Rupert Brooke's "The Soldier," 1–8.
[15] Military term for camping in the open air without tents.
[16] worried
[17] Vimy and Passchendaele were the sites of two battles that had devastating consequences for Canadian troops, but proved successful and bolstered their reputation as gritty and determined soldiers.

A loneliness begot of hours when dreams obsess
With visions of fine ardors[18] and great battle-throes.
These often had he shared with comrades who still keep
The ramparts of dead Freedom safe. Now he no more with them
Shall stand against the battle surge, or sweep
To victory and mark a comrade with death's diadem.[19]
With every wind of war or deathless deed that blows
His spirit chides, his soul self-scathing grows,
To know that he is fated from the fervors of the day,
The great endurances and glories of the fray.   30
Yet gladly would he go—and scorn the utmost cost—
Though he should fall at Arras or at Avion[20] be lost.

Oh, Comrades of mine, who war undauntedly "out there"—
For you this is my inmost wish, my constant prayer:
God stay you through dark day and through red night,
And Christ go with you, triumphing, down to the fight.

                                                         (1919)

Night Witchery in France

I who with ravished eyes, have seen
A thousand homeland Sunsets lay
The lavish glories of their fulvous[21] lights
Before the Dusk; and watched the Moon rise up, serene,
And queenly ride adown her vast highway,
Close-sentinelled and cavalcaded by
 A million stars; or gazed, in wonder, on the ghostly dance
Of rare Aurora Borealis in the Northern sky—

---

[18] passions
[19] crown
[20] Both French towns. Arras was the site of a series of battles; the area around Avion was particularly dangerous and muddy, where thousands of Canadian soldiers died, never to be recovered.
[21] red-yellow colour

I, who have drunk these ever-fresh delights,
Declare the witchery of thy nights,   10
O fair enchantress, France!

A soldier, I, far from my native land
And all the dear, sweet ministries of love,—
I look upon thy battlefields, I look above,
And ask: What commerce can I have with beauty,
Whose times are wholly pledged to deeds of brutal duty?
Yet when I contemplate the placid dome
Of thy nocturnal skies,
My heart turns back to home:
The Moon a mother is, who watches o'er   20
Her little ones, with wise solicitude;
The Stars are all her Children, playing on the floor
Of Heaven; and Dawn, a nurse, both kind and good,
Who takes the mother's stead,
And when they're tired of hide-and-seek, and fed,
Wraps them in downy clouds, and snuggles them in bed.
And so I thank my God, O fair enchantress, France,
For all the witchery of thy nights that stay
Me while I fight to give Christ's little ones the chance,
Upon a peaceful earth, to play.   30

(1919)

John McCrae
(1872–1918)

No anthology of Canadian war poetry would be complete without the work of John McCrae. After volunteering for the Boer War, this native of Guelph, Ontario was a veteran soldier by 1914 and worked as a field surgeon, treating the wounded from some of the war's most vicious battles, including the Second Battle of Ypres. He died of pneumonia in 1918.

In addition to his medical and military work, McCrae was a writer of textbooks, short stories, and poems, and some of those writings appeared in student journals and popular magazines. None of his other writings receive the attention that his most famous poem did. First published in the London-based magazine *Punch*, "In Flanders Fields" quickly became a rallying cry for recruiting efforts, appearing on posters and quoted in speeches, by urging the unsure citizens to not break faith with those who had already died. In the years that followed, the poem played a different role, reminding us of our debts to those who went to war and those who did not come home.

The Anxious Dead

O guns, fall silent till the dead men hear
    Above their heads the legions pressing on:
(These fought their fight in time of bitter fear,
    And died not knowing how the day had gone.)

O flashing muzzles, pause, and let them see
    The coming dawn that streaks the sky afar;
Then let your mighty chorus witness be
    To them, and Caesar, that we still make war.

Tell them, O guns, that we have heard their call,
    That we have sworn, and will not turn aside,   10
That we will onward till we win or fall,
    That we will keep the faith for which they died.

Bid them be patient, and some day, anon,
    They shall feel earth enwrapt in silence deep;
Shall greet, in wonderment, the quiet dawn,
    And in content may turn them to their sleep.

                                          (*1915*, 1919)

In Flanders Fields

In Flanders fields the poppies blow
    Between the crosses, row on row,
    That mark our place; and in the sky
    The larks, still bravely singing, fly
Scarce heard amid the guns below.

We are the Dead. Short days ago
We lived, felt dawn, saw sunset glow,
    Loved and were loved, and now we lie,
        In Flanders fields.

Take up our quarrel with the foe: 10
To you from failing hands we throw
    The torch; be yours to hold it high.
    If ye break faith with us who die
We shall not sleep, though poppies grow
    In Flanders fields.

(*1917*, 1919)

Robert Service

(1874–1958)

By the middle of the twentieth century, Robert Service was one of Canada's (and North America's) most popular and prolific poets, but he began his career as a part-time writer in the isolated climes of northwestern Canada. One of the most popular poets in early twentieth century Canada, Service was first known for his poems of northern adventure. Born to Scottish parents living in Preston, England, Service travelled to the west coast of North America before moving north, first to Whitehorse and then to Dawson City. Working as a banker and moonlighting as a poet, Service wrote verses (as he called them) of rollicking and romantic adventures in his adopted homeland, such as "The Cremation of Sam McGee" and "The Shooting of Dan McGrew" (1907). By the end of his career, Service had achieved a notoriety nearly unheard of for a Canadian poet. He had produced numerous collections of poetry, worked in Hollywood, and travelled extensively in North America and Europe. He was, until the middle of the twentieth century, a crucial figure in any history or anthology of Canadian literature.

During the war, Service worked as an ambulance driver for the Red Cross and a war correspondent for a number of regional newspapers. Most of his war poetry is found in *Rhymes of a Red Cross Man* (1916), an ambivalent and unique collection of poems that earned the poet both praise and derision for its complex and visceral presentation of the war. A bestseller for two years during the war (strangely, in the non-fiction category), *Rhymes of a Red Cross Man* was celebrated by one critic because it gave "a closer sense of life in the great War than any correspondent, novelist, or poet has yet given"[1] and condemned by another as "versified brutalities, or poetical garbage."[2] Despite the success of *Rhymes of a Red Cross Man*, Service would write only one other book about the war. In 1921, he published *Ballads of a Bohemian*, a compilation of prose and poetry that follows the life of troubled protagonist Stephen Poore before and after World War I.

The Call

(*France, August first, 1914*)

Far and near, high and clear,
  Hark to the call of War!
Over the gorse and the golden dells,
Ringing and swinging of clamorous bells,
Praying and saying of wild farewells:
  War! War! War!

High and low, all must go:
  Hark to the shout of War!
Leave to the women the harvest yield;
Gird ye, men, for the sinister field;   10
A sabre instead of a scythe to wield:
  War! Red War!

---

[1] Witter Bynner, "Poetry of the Trenches," review of *Rhymes of a Red Cross Man* by Robert Service, *The Dial* 61 (14 December 1916), 532.
[2] Logan, "Canadian Poetry of the Great War," 412.

Rich and poor, lord and boor,
    Hark to the blast of War!
Tinker and tailor and millionaire,
Actor in triumph and priest in prayer,
Comrades now in the hell out there,
    Sweep to the fire of War!

Prince and page, sot and sage,
    Hark to the roar of War!   20
Poet, professor and circus clown,
Chimney-sweeper and fop o' the town,
Into the pot and be melted down:
    Into the pot of War!

Women all, hear the call,
    The pitiless call of War!
Look your last on your dearest ones,
Brothers and husbands, fathers, sons:
Swift they go to the ravenous guns,
    The gluttonous guns of War.   30

Everywhere thrill the air
    The maniac bells of War.
There will be little of sleeping to-night;
There will be wailing and weeping to-night;
Death's red sickle is reaping to-night:
    War! War! War!

(1916)

The Fool

"But it isn't playing the game," he said,
And he slammed his books away;
"The Latin and Greek I've got in my head
Will do for a duller day."

"Rubbish!" I cried; "The bugle's call
Isn't for lads from school."
D'ye think he'd listen? Oh, not at all:
So I called him a fool, a fool.

Now there's his dog by his empty bed,
And the flute he used to play,   10
And his favourite bat ... but Dick he's dead,
Somewhere in France, they say:
Dick with his rapture of song and sun,
Dick of the yellow hair,
Dicky whose life had but begun,
Carrion-cold out there.

Look at his prizes all in a row:
Surely a hint of fame.
Now he's finished with,—nothing to show:
Doesn't it seem a shame?   20
Look from the window! All you see
Was to be his one day:
Forest and furrow, lawn and lea,
And he goes and chucks it away.

Chucks it away to die in the dark:
Somebody saw him fall,
Part of him mud, part of him blood,
The rest of him—not at all.
And yet I'll bet he was never afraid,
And he went as the best of 'em go,   30
For his hand was clenched on his broken blade,
And his face was turned to the foe.

And I called him a fool ... oh how blind was I!
And the cup of my grief's abrim.
Will Glory o' England ever die
So long as we've lads like him?

So long as we've fond and fearless fools,
Who, spurning fortune and fame,
Turn out with the rallying cry of their schools,
Just bent on playing the game.   40

A fool! Ah no! He was more than wise.
His was the proudest part.
He died with the glory of faith in his eyes,
And the glory of love in his heart.
And though there's never a grave to tell,
Nor a cross to mark his fall,
Thank God! we know that he "batted well"
In the last great Game of all.

(1916)

Foreword[3]

I've tinkered at my bits of rhymes
In weary, woeful, waiting times;
In doleful hours of battle-din,
Ere yet they brought the wounded in;
Through vigils of the fateful night,
In lousy barns by candle-light;
In dug-outs, sagging and aflood,
On stretchers stiff and bleared with blood;
By ragged grove, by ruined road,
By hearths accurst where Love abode;   10
By broken altars, blackened shrines
I've tinkered at my bits of rhymes.

---

[3] This "Foreword" appears at the beginning of *Rhymes of a Red Cross Man* (1916).

I've solaced me with scraps of song
The desolated ways along:
Through sickly fields all shrapnel-sown,
And meadows reaped by death alone;
By blazing cross and splintered spire,
By headless Virgin in the mire;
By gardens gashed amid their bloom,
By gutted grave, by shattered tomb;   20
Beside the dying and the dead,
Where rocket green and rocket red,
In trembling pools of poising light,
With flowers of flame festoon the night.
Ah me! by what dark ways of wrong
I've cheered my heart with scraps of song.

So here's my sheaf of war-won verse,
And some is bad, and some is worse.
And if at times I curse a bit,
You needn't read that part of it;   30
For through it all like horror runs
The red resentment of the guns.
And you yourself would mutter when
You took the things that once were men,
And sped them through that zone of hate
To where the dripping surgeons wait;
And wonder too if in God's sight
War ever, ever can be right.

Yet may it not be, crime and war
But effort misdirected are?   40
And if there's good in war and crime,
There may be in my bits of rhyme,
My songs from out the slaughter mill:
So take or leave them as you will.

                                        (1916)

On the Wire

O God, take the sun from the sky!
It's burning me, scorching me up.
God, can't You hear my cry?
Water! A poor, little cup!
It's laughing, the cursed sun!
See how it swells and swells
Fierce as a hundred hells!
God, will it never have done?
It's searing the flesh on my bones;
It's beating with hammers red   10
My eyeballs into my head;
It's parching my very moans.
See! It's the size of the sky,
And the sky is a torrent of fire,
Foaming on me as I lie
Here on the wire … the wire. …

Of the thousands that wheeze and hum
Heedlessly over my head,
Why can't a bullet come,
Pierce to my brain instead,   20
Blacken forever my brain,
Finish forever my pain?
Here in the hellish glare
Why must I suffer so?
Is it God doesn't care?
Is it God doesn't know?
Oh, to be killed outright,
Clean in the clash of the fight!
That is a golden death,
That is a boon; but this …   30
Drawing an anguished breath
Under a hot abyss,
Under a stooping sky

Of seething, sulphurous fire,
Scorching me up as I lie
Here on the wire ... the wire. ...

Hasten, O God, Thy night!
Hide from my eyes the sight
Of the body I stare and see
Shattered so hideously.   40
I can't believe that it's mine.
My body was white and sweet,
Flawless and fair and fine,
Shapely from head to feet;
Oh no, I can never be
The thing of horror I see
Under the rifle fire,
Trussed on the wire ... the wire. ...

Of night and of death I dream;
Night that will bring me peace,   50
Coolness and starry gleam,
Stillness and death's release:
Ages and ages have passed,—
Lo! it is night at last.
Night! but the guns roar out.
Night! but the hosts attack.
Red and yellow and black
Geysers of doom upspout.
Silver and green and red
Star-shells hover and spread.   60
Yonder off to the right
Fiercely kindles the fight;
Roaring near and more near,
Thundering now in my ear;
Close to me, close ... Oh, hark!
Someone moans in the dark.
I hear, but I cannot see,

I hear as the rest retire,
Someone is caught like me,
Caught on the wire ... the wire. ...   70

Again the shuddering dawn,
Weird and wicked and wan;
Again, and I've not yet gone.
The man whom I heard is dead.
Now I can understand:
A bullet hole in his head,
A pistol gripped in his hand.
Well, he knew what to do,—
Yes, and now I know too. ...

Hark the resentful guns!   80
Oh, how thankful am I
To think my beloved ones
Will never know how I die!
I've suffered more than my share;
I'm shattered beyond repair;
I've fought like a man the fight,
And now I demand the right
(God! how his fingers cling!)
To do without shame this thing.
Good! there's a bullet still;   90
Now I'm ready to fire;
Blame me, God, if You will,
Here on the wire ... the wire. ...

                                                  (1916)

The Revelation

The same old sprint in the morning, boys, to the same old din and smut;
Chained all day to the same old desk, down in the same old rut;

Posting the same old greasy books, catching the same old train:
Oh, how will I manage to stick it all, if I ever get back again?

We've bidden good-bye to life in a cage, we're finished with
     pushing a pen;
They're pumping us full of bellicose rage, they're showing us how
     to be men.
We're only beginning to find ourselves; we're wonders of brawn
     and thew;[4]
But when we go back to our Sissy jobs,—oh, what are we going to
     do?

For shoulders curved with the counter stoop will be carried erect
     and square;
And faces white from the office light will be bronzed by the open
     air;   10
And we'll walk with the stride of a new-born pride, with a
     new-found joy in our eyes,
Scornful men who have diced with death under the naked skies.

And when we get back to the dreary grind, and the bald-headed
     boss's call,
Don't you think that the dingy window-blind, and the dingier
     office wall,
Will suddenly melt to a vision of space, of violent, flame-scarred
     night?
Then ... oh, the joy of the danger-thrill, and oh, the roar of the
     fight!

Don't you think as we peddle a card of pins the counter will fade
     away,
And again we'll be seeing the sand-bag rims, and the barb-wire's
     misty grey?

---

4   physical powers like strength and vigour

As a flat voice asks for a pound of tea, don't you fancy we'll hear
    instead
The night-wind moan and the soothing drone of the packet that's
    overhead?   20

Don't you guess that the things we're seeing now will haunt us
    through all the years;
Heaven and hell rolled into one, glory and blood and tears;
Life's pattern picked with a scarlet thread, where once we wove
    with a grey
To remind us all how we played our part in the shock of an epic
    day?

Oh, we're booked for the Great Adventure now, we're pledged to
    the Real Romance;
We'll find ourselves or we'll lose ourselves somewhere in giddy
    old France;
We'll know the zest of the fighter's life; the best that we have we'll
    give;
We'll hunger and thirst; we'll die ... but first—we'll live; by the
    gods, we'll live!

We'll breathe free air and we'll bivouac[5] under the starry sky;
We'll march with men and we'll fight with men, and we'll see
    men laugh and die;   30
We'll know such joy as we never dreamed; we'll fathom the
    deeps of pain:
But the hardest bit of it all will be—when we come back home
    again.

For some of us smirk in a chiffon shop, and some of us teach in a
    school;
Some of us help with the seat of our pants to polish an office stool;

---

[5]   Military term for camping in the open air without tents.

The merits of somebody's soap or jam some of us seek to explain,
But all of us wonder what we'll do when we have to go back again.

(1916)

The Stretcher-Bearer

My stretcher is one scarlet stain,
And as I tries to scrape it clean,
I tell you wot—I'm sick with pain
For all I've 'eard, for all I've seen;
Around me is the 'ellish night,
And as the war's red rim I trace,
I wonder if in 'Eaven's height,
Our God don't turn away 'Is Face.

I don't care 'oose the Crime may be;
I 'olds no brief for kin or clan;   10
I 'ymns no 'ate: I only see
As man destroys his brother man;
I waves no flag: I only know,
As 'ere beside the dead I wait,
A million 'earts is weighed with woe,
A million 'omes is desolate.

In drippin' darkness, far and near,
All night I've sought them woeful ones.
Dawn shudders up and still I 'ear
The crimson chorus of the guns.   20
Look! like a ball of blood the sun
'Angs o'er the scene of wrath and wrong. ...
"Quick! Stretcher-bearers on the run!"
O Prince of Peace! 'Ow long, 'ow long?

(1916)

F.O. Call
(1878–1956)

———◆———

Born in West Brome, Quebec, Frank Oliver Call studied in Montreal, Paris, and Switzerland before returning to a professorship at Bishop's College in Lennoxville, Quebec. As a poet, Call was one of Canada's early modernists, a reputation he earned as a result of his extended defence of *vers libre* in the foreword to *Acanthus and Wild Grape* (1920). A way of writing poetry without the conventional metres and predictable rhythms, *vers libre* is a hallmark of Anglo-American modernist innovation and, in Call's estimation, a durable and necessary feature of early twentieth-century poetry: "like the motor-car and aeroplane, [*vers libre*] has come to stay whether we like it or no."[1] While scholars debate the intensity of Call's commitment to modernism (his poetry is better thought of as transitional, rather than fully fledged), there can be little doubt that his poetry had its admirers. As late as 1939, A.J.M. Smith declared Call one of our literature's "careful craftsmen," and among the "best" writers of Canadian poetry.[2]

Very few of Call's war poems take advantage of the potential energies of *vers libre*. Instead, Call chooses more traditional verse forms with predictable metres and line-endings, features that oppose the chaos and disharmony of a war-torn world.

---

[1] F.O. Call, foreword to *Acanthus and Wild Grape* (Toronto: McClelland & Stewart, 1920), 10.
[2] A.J.M. Smith, "Canadian Poetry—A Minority Report," *University of Toronto Quarterly* 8, no. 2 (1939): 133

Calvary

The women stood and watched while thick, black night
    Enclosed the awful tragedy. Afar
      Three crosses stood, against a single bar
Of crimson-glowing, black-encircled light.
No hint of Easter dawn. In all the height
    Of that dark heaven, not a single star
      To whisper;—Love and Life the victors are.
It seemed to them that wrong had conquered right.

O ye who watch and wait, the night is long.
A curtain of spun fire and woven gloom   10
      Across the mighty tragedy is drawn.
But soon your ears shall hear a triumph song,
    And golden light shall touch each sacred tomb,
      And voices shout at last—The Dawn! The Dawn.

AUGUST, 1916.

(1917)

In a Belgian Garden

Once in a Belgian garden,
    (Ah, many months ago!)
I saw like pale Madonnas
    The tall white lilies blow.

Great poplars swayed and trembled
    Afar against the sky,
And green with flags and rushes
    The river wandered by.

Amid the waving wheatfields
    Glowed poppies blazing red.   10

And showering strange wild music
　A lark rose overhead.

*　　*　　*

The lark has ceased his singing,
　The wheat is trodden low,
And in the blood-stained garden
　No more the lilies blow.

And where green poplars trembled
　Stand shattered trunks instead.
And lines of small white crosses
　Keep guard above the dead.　　　　　　　　　20

For here brave lads and noble,
　From lands beyond the deep,
Beneath the small white crosses
　Have laid them down to sleep.

They laid them down with gladness
　Upon the alien plain.
That this same Belgian garden
　Might bud and bloom again.

(1917)

The Indifferent Ones

Unmoved they sit by the stream of life
　And its blood-red tide to the sea goes down,
While the hosts are borne through the surging strife
　To a hero's death and a martyr's crown.

They pay no toll of their gold or blood;
　For them 'tis a pageant and naught beside;

So they calmly dream by the reeking flood,
    While the sun goes down in the crimson tide.

(1917)

The Lace-Maker of Bruges[3]

Her age-worn hands upon her apron lie
    Idle and still. Against the sunset glow
    Tall poplars stand and silent barges go
Along the green canal that wanders by.
A lean, red finger pointing to the sky.
    The spire of Notre Dame. Above a row
Of dim, gray arches where the sunbeams die.
    The ancient belfry guards the square below.

One August eve she stood in that same square
    And gazed and listened, proud beneath her tears.   10
        To see her soldier passing down the street.
To-night the beat of drums and trumpets' blare
    With bursts of fiendish music smite her ears.
        And mingle with the tread of trampling feet.

(1917)

Gone West[4]
Dedicated to Lieutenant Rodolphe Lemieux,
killed in action August 29, 1918.

I do not think of them—our glorious dead—
    As laying tired heads upon the breast
    Of a kind mother to be lulled to rest;
I do not see them in a narrow bed

---

[3]   Historic city in Belgium held by the Germans.
[4]   euphemism for dying or death

Of alien earth by their own blood dyed red,
　But see in their own simple phrase—Gone West—
　The words of knights upon a holy quest,
Who saw the light and followed where it led.

Gone West! Scarred warrior hosts go marching by,
　Their longing faces turned to greet the light　　10
That glows and burns upon the western sky.
　Leaving behind the darkness of the night,
The long day over and the battle won,
They seek for rest beyond the setting sun.

(1920)

To a Modern Poet

Why must you sing of sorrow
　When the world is so full of woe?
Why must you sing of the ugly?
　For the ugly and sad I know.
Why will you sing of railways,
　Of Iron and Steel and Coal,
And the din of the smoky cities?
　For these will not feed my soul.

But sing to me songs of beauty
　To gladden my tired eyes,—　　10
The beauty of waving forest,
　Of meadows and sunlit skies;
Sing me of childish laughter,
　Of cradles and painted toys,
Of the sea and the brooks and the rivers,
　And the shouting of bathing boys.

For the earth has a store of beauty
　Deep hid from our blinded eyes,

And only the true-born poet
    Knows just where the treasure lies.   20
So lead me from paths that are ugly,
    From the dust of the city street.
To paths that are fringed with flowers,
    Where the sky and the meadows meet.

And though Sorrow may walk beside me
    To the far, far end of the road,
If Beauty but beckon me onward,
    Less heavy will seem my load;
And led in the paths of beauty,
    The world from its strife will cease;   30
For I know that the paths of beauty
    Lead on to the paths of peace.

                (1920)

Katherine Hale

(1878–1956)

Katherine Hale (a pseudonym for Amelia Warnock) was born in Galt, Ontario, married editor John W. Garvin, and became a popular and, according to some, influential writer and critic for Toronto's *Mail and Empire*. Her war poetry collections—three in total—brought her popular success (earning her glowing reviews in the city's newspapers), but it wasn't until her later volumes of poetry that she would be praised by her fellow poets Charles G.D. Roberts and J.D. Logan.

Some of Hale's war poems are just as critic Wanda Campbell describes: "sentimental and patriotic poetry of the home front."[1] Her descriptions of battlefields stay true to the ideals of heroism and national glory. Perhaps more successful (or at least more affecting)

---

[1] Wanda Campbell, "Moonlight to Morning: Women's Early Contribution to Canadian Modernism," in *The Canadian Modernists Meet*, ed. Dean Irvine (Ottawa: University of Ottawa Press, 2005), 86.

are those that focus on a woman's relationship with the war, her distance from the battlefield, her fantasies about the return of her loved ones, and her secret struggles against the darker days.

Grey Knitting[2]

All through the country, in the autumn stillness,
A web of grey spreads strangely, rim to rim;
And you may hear the sound of knitting needles,
Incessant, gentle,—dim.

A tiny click of little wooden needles,
Elfin amid the gianthood of war;
Whispers of women, tireless and patient,
Who weave the web afar.

Whispers of women, tireless and patient—
'Foolish, inadequate!' we hear you say;   10
'Grey wool on fields of hell is out of fashion,'
And yet we weave the web from day to day.

Suppose some soldier dying, gaily dying,
Under the alien skies, in his last hour,
Should listen, in death's prescience so vivid,
And hear a fairy sound bloom like a flower—

I like to think that soldiers, gaily dying
For the white Christ on fields with shame sown deep,
May hear the fairy click of women's needles,
As they fall fast asleep.   20
                                                          (1914)

---

[2]   During the war, many women on the home front spent time knitting clothes to be sent to soldiers serving in Europe.

When You Return

When you return I see the radiant street,
I hear the rushing of a thousand feet,
I see the ghosts that women come to greet.

I can feel roses, roses all the way,
The fearful gladness that no power can stay,
The joy that glows and grows in ambient ray.

Because slim lads come marching home from war?
Truly, slim lads, home from Very Far:
From fields as distant as the farthest star.

It will be strange to hear the plaudits roll,   10
Back from that zone where soul is flung on soul,
Where they go out like sparks to one straight goal.

Where souls go out as fast as moments fly,
Urging their claim on the unbending sky—
Surely it must be wonderful to die!

        *   *   *

When you return I see the radiant street,
I hear the rushing of a thousand feet—
Living and Dead with roses we shall greet.

(1914)

You Who Have Gayly Left Us

You who have gaily left us youth-beshorn,
The town is sunless and the roof forlorn;
Dread stands beside the pillow every morn.

But glory is a beacon in the night,
So brilliant that it bathes the world in light,
And lures these slim lads marching out to fight.

Country of mine, so very strong and young,
What of dark banners fast before you flung?
What of the awful battles yet unsung?

No joyous road I ask for you to-day,   10
I dare not pipe you peace along the way
That leads to Darkness or increasing Day.

For Heaven plays the prelude: drum and fife
Merging the morning into larger life
Challenge the noon of banners and of strife;

Until, within the living crimson flame,
There seems to burn a new-born country's name,
The Friend of Light, and Honor's deathless fame.

(1914)

The Awakening

How like a giant stretching in the sun,
We have slept through the ages;[3] even we
Whom the gods moulded from a people free,
And made tremendous for the race not run.

See we have slept a magic cycle round,
And in the dream we have imagined much;

---

[3]   Cf. Rupert Brooke's "Peace" (1914): "Now, God be thanked Who has matched us with His
hour, / And caught our youth, and wakened us from sleeping, / With hand made sure, clear
eye, and sharpened power, / To turn, as swimmers into cleanness leaping" (1–4).

Felt the soft wings of years we did not touch,
Dallied with somnolence that deadens sound.

With untried strength what we have done is done.
The wandering, drowsy brain has vaguely stirred,   10
As though from out infinitude it heard
A great voice speaking from behind the sun.

Closer and clear the calling, strangely loud,
And the great country, rousing from long sleep
Murmurs to its own soul, as deep to deep
Beckons a day's new dawn, so sure and proud.

These were the visions of a passing night,
Visions now caught in bugle notes of flame,
And lo, through storms of war we hear our name
Called by an angel, terrible and bright!   20

(1916)

The Hearts of Mothers

The hearts of mothers are hid things
In these the days of woe,
And troops of strange thoughts move therein
Silently to and fro.

They are not thoughts of yester-year,
Or thoughts of you and me
And that which we have done, or do,
By air, or land, or sea.

But these are thoughts steel-bright with pain,
And death-thoughts bare and stark,   10
And shining thoughts of armaments
That glitter through the dark.

They move, old passions and revolts,
Fresh-called, yet stiff with scars,
To music crimsoned with the clash
Of endless ancient wars.

And those who summon memories
From pathways of the sun,
When death spoke life most solemnly
Ere new life was begun,   20

They dream of a strange blooming
That dawns in greater birth:
The frail, bright flower of selflessness
Brought back again to earth.

They feel, the Givers of all Life,
Great need to give again
The utmost dower of womanhood,
All mystery—all pain.

                                                            (1916)

Soul of the Earth

I saw a tired soldier vainly searching
For room to bury deeply the new dead.
"The old dead they are there, forever perching
About the space we need," he grimly said.
"The old dead, slaughtered, just beneath the sod
Of Earth that once was well-beloved of God."

I heard a woman desperate in her wooing
Of empty space and echoing aisles of air,
Calling upon the gods of her undoing
To stem the fearful flood of her despair.   10

"Somewhere in France he lies so deep," she said.
"That Earth must make me answer for my dead."

And all the while a wondrous bloom was springing
Above the fields where lie these broken boys,
Thousands of souls like butterflies upwinging
In troop on radiant troop of shining joys.
Host upon host they seek eternal breath
Above the little mounds of lonely death.

"Thus," saith the Earth, "my poppies pass in splendour,
Flame of young hearts, for still my world is young,   20
And in great Ages, wise because more tender,
The passion of their passing shall be sung.
As of these Ages! For the soul of me
Know endless blooming—vivid, changing, free."

                                        (1916)

Wilson MacDonald

(1880–1967)

Wilson MacDonald is now remembered for his vigorous self-promotion and his constant touring; but there was a time when he was also known as a writer who was standing on the cutting edge of poetry. Some critics (mostly his admiring contemporaries and residents of his hometown of Cheapside, Ontario, which still maintains a museum named in his honour) were eager to insist that MacDonald was a new kind of writer; others saw his experiments as too timid, too fully invested in the conventions of an era long gone.

It would be wrong to suggest that MacDonald's war poems—or his other poems, for that matter—are anything but traditional in form or content. But what separates a poem like "The Girl Behind the Man Behind the Gun" (1915) from some of the other poems published early in the war (see especially the war song, "It's the Man Behind the Gun that Does the Work" [1915]) is the poem's persistent focus on women's wartime experiences—work, suffering, and personal sacrifices.

The Girl Behind the Man Behind the Gun

You have seen the line of khaki swinging grandly down the street.
    You have heard the band blare out Brittanic songs.
You have read a ton of papers, and you've thrown them at your feet;
    And your brain's a battle-field for fighting throngs.
You have cheered for Tommy Atkins and you've yelled for Jack Canuck;
    You have praised the French and Belgians, every one.
But I'm rhyming here a measure to the valor and the pluck
    Of the girl behind the man behind the gun.

There's a harder game than fighting; there's a deeper wound by far
    Than the bayonet or the bullet ever tore.   10

And a patient little woman wears upon her heart a scar.
    Which the lonesome years will keep for evermore.
There are bands and bugles crying, and the horses madly ride;
    And in passion are the trenches lost or won.
But SHE battles in the silence, with no comrade at her side,
    Does the girl behind the man behind the gun.

They are singing songs in Flanders, and there's laughter on the wind;
    They are shouting for their country and their king.
But the hallways yearn for music in the homes they left behind;
    For the mother of a soldier does not sing.   20
In the silence of the night time, mid a ring of hidden foes,
    And without a bugle cry to cheer her on,
She is fighting fiercer battles than a soldier ever known;
    And her triumph is an open grave, at dawn.

You have cheered the line of khaki swinging grandly down the street;
    But you quite forgot to cheer another line.
They are plodding sadly homeward, with no music for their feet,
    To a far more lonely river than the Rhine.[1]
Ah! the battle field is wider than the cannon's sullen roar;
    And the women weep o'er battles lost or won.   30
For the man a cross of honor; but the crepe upon the door[2]
    For the girl behind the man behind the gun.

When the heroes are returning and the world with flags is red;
    When they show the tattered trophies of the war;
When your cheers are for the living and your tears for the dead,
    Which the foeman in the battle trampled o'er;
When you fling your reddest roses at the horseman in array,
    With their helmets flaming proudly in the sun,

---

[1] River running through Germany and connecting a number of European countries.
[2] Sign that there has been a death in the family.

I would bid you wear the favour of an apple blossom spray,
  For the girl behind the man behind the gun.   40

January 14th, 1915, Victoria, B.C.

                                                          (1915)

E.J. Pratt
(1882–1964)

Born in Western Bay, Newfoundland, E.J. Pratt spent most of his young adult life studying, teaching, and writing in Toronto before moving to Victoria. Pratt is usually thought of as a transitional figure in Canadian literature, part traditionalist (with an interest in older forms and features like the narrative poem or the heroic couplet) and part modernist (with an interest in images and ideas of industry and science). His war poetry is no exception—sometimes offering comfort and consolation in the form of traditional elegies, sometimes revelling in the violent imagery of the trenches, and sometimes reverting to narratives of hope and renewal. Whatever the case, there can be no doubt that the war had a serious personal impact on Pratt. As scholars have pointed out, he was deeply affected by the death of a fellow student (for which he wrote "Dead on the Field of Honour" [1916]),[1] the drowning of his brother, and the near total destruction of Newfoundland's First Battalion in 1916, at the beginning of the Battle of the Somme.

---

[1] "Timeline," *The Complete Poems of E.J. Pratt: A Hypertext Edition*, eds. Sandra Djwa and Zailig Pollack, Trent University, Peterborough, 18 March 2009 <http://www.trentu.ca/faculty/pratt/>.

Dead on the Field of Honour[2]

"Dead on the field of Honour." Came the words
In slow pulsation on the printed page,
And April with her buds and happy birds
Became November, with her ash and age.

"Dead on the field of Honour." Pale the face
That gazes on me in my fitful dreams,
And alien forms within the gloom I trace
Beside the hallowed body, as it seems.

"Dead on the field of Honour." Let it be.
With Glory's paeans sounding let us part   10
'Tis meet that Honour's tribute should be free,
But cloistered grief keeps tolling in my heart.

(1916)

The Largess of 1917

Our eyes were open but we did not see,
Our ears unstopped, and yet we did not hear;
The thunders of the world's great agony,
The lightnings of its dread unmeasured fear,
Had made us blind and deaf, and though our hand
Had often touched the satin of a flower,
In the June splendour of a noon-tide hour,
We could not feel: we could not understand.

---

[2] This poem was written on the occasion of the death of Victoria College student-turned-soldier John Lumsden; "Timeline," *The Complete Poems of E.J. Pratt: A Hypertext Edition*, eds. Sandra Djwa and Zailig Pollock, Trent University, Peterborough, 18 March 2009 <http:www.trentu.ca/faculty/pratt/>.

Three years had drifted by, and we were old,
The crust had fallen; how? we could not tell.   10
The pulse had slowed, the heart was strangely cold,
Youth disenchanted long had lost its spell;
Yet children told us what they saw and heard—
With blue-orbed wonder in their open eyes,
Before the lifted wand of heaven's skies—
In blush of flower, and in song of bird.

And older ones and wiser far than we,
Whose steps had turned to childhood paths once more,
Whose feet had neared the marge[3] of that great sea
Where tideless waters bathe a crystal shore,   20
These—pilgrims near God's shrine—had told us too,
Of rays with which the sun the clouds had lined,
Of fragrance and of music in the wind,
Of glories bursting as the seasons flew;

Of winter fashioning some sunlit palace,
Chiselling the spires of some marble fane,[4]
Pouring rich sunlight from a golden chalice,
Or frosting petals on a window-pane;
Of virginal white of firs ere rough winds shake
The trembling vesture of their limbs of snow;   30
Of stars, the bright moon's crescent underglow,
Beneath the silver panels of a lake.

Come spring; and life, they said, in myriad form
Arose, buoyant, effulgent,[5] crowned with light,
Life issuing from darkness, death and storm,
Dawn floating from the bosom of the night;

---

[3]   edge; in this case, shore
[4]   temple
[5]   radiant, brilliant

Life's colours all unfurled upon the land,
Life's music beating on the resonant air,
Life—sandaled on the waters everywhere;
And yet, we did not see, nor understand.   40

The summer called. 'Twas answered by the thrush,
The dance of daisies in their matchless grace,
The gold of buttercup, the passionate blush
Of damask rose, the lily's chastened face.
This did they see, which yet was but a part
Of what they saw—they could not tell the whole—
The rose had whispered something to the soul,
The lily sent a challenge to the heart.

Autumn! and sunrise on the mountain-steep,
The wine of morning, sweet and brimming cool,   50
The stainless fleece of cirrus-clouds that sleep
In the hushed beauty of a dreaming pool,
The molten amber of a sea becalmed,
When eve draws nigh, and in the star-swept nights,
The mystic archery of Northern lights,
God's martial hosts advancing, angel-psalmed.

And when the fall's last petals had been shed,
When the last robin's song had taken wing,
When colours faded, and life's glories fled,
They told us that they saw a fairer thing;   60
—Those pilgrims toiling on earth's dusted sod—
The beckoning home-lure of the Westering ray,
Heaven's candle lighted at the close of day,
The hearth-fires of their Father and their God.

(1918)

Before a Bulletin Board
(*After Beaumont-Hamel*)[6]

God! How should letters change their colours so?
    A little *k* or *m* stab like a sword;[7]
How dry, black ink should turn to red and flow,
    And figures leap like hydras[8] on the board?

A woman raised her voice, and she was told
    That strange things happen at the will of God;
Thus, dawn from midnight; thus, from fire the gold;
    Thus did a rose once blossom from a rod.[9]

But stranger things today, than that the rod
    Should flower, or the cross become a crown—   10
Stranger than gold from fire; else how should God
    Bring on the night before the sun go down.

        (1923)

From A Fragment from a Story

I

(Thaddeus, a traveller, speaking to Julian,
an old man)

      … Fields far and near,
Hills, ridges, valleys, lowlands, marsh and plain,

---

6 Small village in northern France that was a location of the Battle of the Somme in 1916, which was devastating for the British troops and their allies, particularly the Newfoundland regiment.
7 "K" and "m" stand for "killed" or "missing." E.J. Pratt, *E.J. Pratt: Complete Poems*, eds. Sandra Djwa and R.G. Moyles. 2 vols. (Toronto: University of Toronto Press, 1989).
8 Serpent-like and deadly beast with many heads (Greek mythology).
9 Three biblical allusions to acts of God in Numbers and Exodus (Dwja and Moyles).

Far to the horizon's utmost rim were filled
With clashing millions. All earth's tribes
Had by some common instinct gathered there,
Peopling the shadows of the awful zone—
The forest shades, the fissures of great rocks,
And caverns cut within the rotted mold;
Each nation's youth, its lithest, strongest, best,
Closed up the crimson rendezvous. The streams   10
That ran their livid washings through the clefts
Of spade or nature's highways, fouled and choked
With drifted foliage of a year grown old,
Too soon, with autumn's hectic leaves and limbs,
And sheddings rare of dearer castaways.
As leaves fall, so upon the plains fell men;
Some tossed awhile within the gust of combat,
High on the sweltered air, returned to earth
As flesh and blood and bone unrecognized,
And indistinguishable dust. Some swayed,   20
Not knowing why they did, as if a breath
Of unnamed pestilence had touched their senses,
Robbed them of aim and guidance. Thus they drooped
And fell; and others could not die till hours
Wore into days and nights. Restless they moved,
And shuddered; clutched convulsively at stones
Or roots, and clenched their teeth upon their hands,
Stifling their moans. And lads of growing years,
Who pain or weariness had never known,
Lay in strange sleep upon the fields, alone,   30
Or huddled up in ghastly heaps where death
Had flung them. Night winds gambolled[10] with their hair,
Golden and brown and dark—they heeded not.
And far along the distant battle lines—
Movements as various as the tides, the rise,

---

[10] frolicked, played

The flow, the swift recessions of despair;
Huge gaps that rendered void the toil of years.
The lines re-formed and the price paid; strong men
Who lunged and parried thrusts and lunged again,
Struck and were struck, unknown to each the foes,   40
Save in the general quarrel and its cause.
And through the lulls of intermittent fight
Was blown death's bitterest music—the low sob
Of brothers mourning brothers dead, the curse
Of fallen men that had not seen their foes,
The unavailing moan that answers moan
At night in the fair comradeship of wounds.
Then, strangest of all sights, the harvest moon
A moment broke through the misty cloud, and shed
Upon the fields a sickly, yellow light,   50
Disclosing pallid faces, blue, strained lips,
And eyes that stared, amazed, through open lids
That had no time to shut—that looked and asked
But one eternal question. Then the moon
Grew dimmer as the mist increased, and showed,
In hazy outlines, hurrying forms that moved
In twos and threes, from place to place, and laid
Upon the stretchers, one by one, the dead,
Torn, jagged, mud-smeared and crumpled, carrying them
To rows of damp deep trenches, newly dug,   60
Where they were placed in groups of eight or ten,
In order, side by side, and face to face—
And the moon shone full again—the harvest moon.

Julian
Your words would tax the heart's belief. I thought
That here along these shores when, at the close
Of a week of storm, the gull alone remained
Upon the waters, and the blinds were drawn
Within a hundred homes, that there was left
On earth nothing that might out-range the winds.

Thaddeus
Death—Death stalked everywhere on land and sea,   70
In clouds that banked the sun, in mists that hid
The stars, or half-disclosed the swollen moon.
No cavern sunk beneath the earth but bore
His foot-prints. Deep below the waters' rim
Great fish had trailed his scent. Earth's myriad forms
Had felt the plague-spot of his rampant touch,
From the small field-mouse, caught within the fumes
Of sulphurous air that crept from knoll to knoll,
Withering the grass blades, to the giant fighter
Of storm and wave that, ribbed and sheathed with steel,   80
Felt the swift scorpion in her sides, then rocked
And plunged with bellowing nostrils till she sank
In a wild litany of guns, with wind,
And night, and flame. But busier was his hand
With subtler workmanship. On eye and brow
And cheek were delved the traces of his passing—
Blindness, that like a thunder-clap at noon,
Closed on the sight; furrows that struck the veins,
Turning the red sap from its wonted course;
Sharp lines of pain and fury and quick hate   90
That on the instant changed to graven stone,
Callous and motionless. And deadlier still,
With flying leap he strode a continent,
Or the wide prairies of a sea, and snatched
The cup from the wan fingers of a life
That slaked its thirst upon the wine of hope;
So sure his hand—light, as with finger-tips,
He touched the hair and wove the grey and white
Within the brown, or hard, with rough-spurred heel,
He mauled the bosom till its heavings ceased.   100

Julian
Where ever in its course was this wide world
So plunged in an unmeasured desolation?

What tenders offered, save in a fool's faith,
Would gamble on the chance of raising it
From the complete involvement of its ruin?

Thaddeus
Many there were who, clutching at a straw
Of some dark saying of the past, some tone,
Or flash of eye carrying strange emphasis,
Sought for the battered remnants of their faith
An anchorage; and around a clay-damp grave   110
That buried hope with dust would stoop to tie
Their heartstrings to a pansy, murmuring thus:
'Who bade this flower renew its own fair lease
Of youth perennial? Springs it not this year
From the same soil and root, with that same pride
With which a year ago it lifted up
Its face before the sun? Does not each year
Declare its trumpet-pledges at the spring?"

Julian
Think they so to convince the heart with words
Like those, to mesh it with a logic meet   120
For bloodless ends? What though the winds of May
Call to the springing rootlets, lure the bud
From the rose-stem, and chase the resinous sap
From the pine's trunk to branch and topmost twig—
Who yields to such delusion? Does the spring
Forget November's hecatombs,[11] the last
Convulsion of the leaf, the gale-torn limbs
Of trees scarred to the death, the flowers that danced
Upon the fields scythed by the autumn's hands—
The written spectres of earth's quick decay   130

---

[11]   Ancient Greek sacrifice to the gods, usually of a hundred cattle; a destruction of high numbers
       (of people or things).

Flashed out upon the winds? All these as dust
Around the season's tombs—dust-heaps, no more;
As sands that eddy in the desert, these:
For these no resurrection. What amends
Does summer make for winter's numbing stroke?
It's death he gives, not slumber. His pale forms
Breathe not again, and eyelids that have closed
On the congealing air reflect no more
The warm glance of the sun. The swallows build
Their nests once more within the eaves; the thrush,   140
The red-breast and the lark cover again
Their young in bush and tree and meadow-grain—
They have not died. But weak ones that, impaled
Upon the thorn, screamed out their notes of pain,
Or dashed, wing-broken, by the wildering[12] blast,
Fell when their strength had failed them on far plains,
On treeless hills, or dazed in homeward flight,
Fluttered and sank in furrows of the sea—
Their song has ended; *they* return no more.

(1923)

---

[12] disorienting

Douglas Leader Durkin

(1884–1967)

Born in Parry Sound, Ontario, Durkin soon moved to rural Manitoba with his family, where he would later study and teach. After falling in love with one of his students (the soon-to-be-writer Martha Ostenso), Durkin moved to New York and wrote and collaborated on a number of novels, short stories, and plays.

Aside from his collaborations with Ostenso, Durkin is best known for his penultimate novel, *The Magpie* (1923)—which he completed while in New York. This work of fiction, later subtitled, *A Novel of Post-War Disillusionment*, follows former-soldier Craig Forrester as he seeks out what he calls "a new sense of justice, a new intelligence, a different order."[1] What Forrester discovers is that the new order that he fought so hard for does not yet exist in Canada. The home front does not live up to the ideals of fairness, democracy, liberty, and prosperity that he thought the war would defend and instill. Durkin's only collection of poetry, *The Fighting Men of Canada* (1918), gives voice to some of the same pre-war idealism that Craig Forrester had. In a number of these poems, war is a chance to confirm individual strength and communal glory; in others, we see Durkin's interest in the wartime roles of men and women.

---

[1]   Douglas Leader Durkin, *The Magpie* (Toronto: Hodder & Stoughton, 1923), 14.

The Call

Came once a call on the midnight,
   Rose once a cry from the sea,
"Daughter of mine in my day-pride,
   Art thou still daughter to me?"
Spoke then the heart of a nation,
   Clarion-voiced from the hill,
"Lo, in our day thou hast long been our stay,
   Mother art thou to us still!"

Came then a murmur of voices,
   Sounds of the marching of men;   10
Hearts that had slumbered in silence
   Quickened with passion again;
Down where the rumble of traffic
   Grew with the dawn of the day
Broke the stern beat of a drum in the street,
   Marshalling men for the fray.

Cold-hearted stewards of credit,
   Faint-hearted counters of pelf,[2]
Leaped at the blare of the trumpet
   Free from the shackles of self;   20
Haggling tongues on the market,
   Babbling lips on the square,
Fashion'd a word that the high heavens heard,
   Whispered it once in a prayer.

Silent-tongued dwellers on frontiers,
   Peace-loving souls on the grange,
Brawny-limbed brood of the mountains,

---

[2] pejorative term for money

Weather-bronzed sons of the range,
Stout-hearted hewers of forests,
  Brown-beaten men of the soil   30
Heard from afar the grim challenge of war—
  Rose in the sweat of their toil.

Back went the word from a people
  Bred with a will to be free,
"Mother, thy daughter stands ready
  Still to prove daughter to thee!"
Spoke then the heart of the Mother,
  Swelling with pride in her Day,
"Soul of my soul, where the battle-clouds roll,
  We are one soul in the fray!"   40

(1918)

Carry On!

Is the game all up, are the boys all in?
  Never mind, old man—carry on!
Have you met defeat where you thought to win?
  Play up, old man—carry on!
Are your eyes a-swim in a blinding sun?
Are your best men crippled, your team-mates done?
Are the wagers against you, five to one?
  Buck up, old man! Carry on! Carry on!

Are you groggy and dazed at the close of the round?
  Come back, old man—carry on!   10
Jump in and mix it, and hold your ground—
  That's it, old man—carry on!
Do you wish like sin that the match was through?
All right—your man may be all in too—
He's probably bluffing the same as you;
  Lead out, old man! Carry on! Carry on!

Is your line in the air and your colonel dead?
    All right, old man—carry on!
Are your picked men shattered and plugged with lead?
    What odds, old man?—carry on!   20
Lie low, hold on, keep pegging away—
It's grit that counts in the game you play,
And it's grit, after all, that wins the day—
    Stand to, old man! Carry on! Carry on!

                                              (1918)

The Father Speaks

I

I have asked myself, yes, every day
Since he gripped my hand and hurried away,
"If the news should come that the lad was dead,
How would you take it?" And I have said,
(To myself of course), "Ah, my heart would break,
But I'd do my best for his mother's sake!"

II

For a man's a man, you see, and I—
Well, times will come when a man must lie;
And I said to myself, "I will lie to her,
And she'll never see with her eyes a-blur   10
From the tears in them—and she'll never know."
    And I thought to myself that I'd maybe go
    Away by myself somewhere and sit
    Alone awhile; and if for a bit
    I quit the struggle and bowed my head
    And wept for loneliness, "Well," I said,
    "What odds? No one will the wiser be,
    No one will know but God and me."

III

And then—it came. The lad was dead.
"*Killed in action*," the message said.   20

IV

That was days ago, and I haven't slept
One hour since—and I've scarcely wept,
For I've not been sad—and my heart is light—
And I've not been lonely. For every night
I have seen him here; he has talked with me;
And all day long he has walked with me;
And every day in the crowded street,
Where go the busy, hurrying feet
Of the shuffling crowd, I have felt him near
Freeing my soul of a nameless Fear.   30

V

But a man's a man, and the heart will fail,
And the days grow stern, and the lights grow pale;
And the night comes down when faith goes out,
And the soul gropes blind in a maze of doubt.

VI

And the hour will come, as it came to me
Just yestereve, when we cannot see
Why the thing we planned must never grow
Into the thing we hoped for. So—
Last night it came. I remembered how
When the lad was small I had touched his brow   40
Where he lay asleep in his little bed,
Weary from play. And my heart had fed
Greedily then with a foolish pride,
And a foolish joy that I could not hide
From his mother's eyes, on the future when

The lad would stand in a world of men
Playing a man's full part. And I lay
Last night—all night—till the rising day
Broke in the east—and I could not sleep
And I watched the grey day slowly creep   50
Over a cold world lately dead,
And the long grey shafts that slowly spread
Over a cold sky. And I cried
Out of a heart where hope had died,
"No rising day and no dawn for me!"
For life was dark and I could not see
Through the heavy mists, and I looked abroad
On a cheerless world where there was no God.

VII

Then in the silence I bowed and wept
For the lad that was gone. But a Presence crept   60
Close to my side and there fell a word
So soft, so still, that I scarcely heard,
"Why weepest thou in the night for me?
Dost thou recall when I went from thee
Smiling to take a man's full share
And render a man's account? 'Twas there
Life's morning broke like a day new born
Out of the clouds of night, and morn
Came on my soul. Did you miss it then—
Miss the meaning of life, that men   70
Who are men indeed must come to know
Somewhere, sometime, if they ever grow
Into the stature that God ordains,
Or free themselves of the sordid chains
That weigh like lead? There is work to do
For men that are men, for such as you
Whose sons have gone up the long white trail
Over the hilltops, past the pale
Of earthly vision. Count it joy

That somewhere undaunted stood a boy   80
Who was flesh of your flesh, who knew the thrill
Of the crowded moment and strove to fill
His last sweet hour with something true
To the blood he boasted. Only the few
Have lived supremely. Take his word
That over the shock of the battle he heard
His father's voice that bade him stand,
Felt the strength of his sire's hand
Double the strength of his own, and died
Unconquered still. Know that his pride   90
Was ever in this, that his record proved
He had accounted the life he loved
Only less dear than honor. Then
Turn to the task of your day again,
Heart-high, soul-strong, with a living will
Mounting the height and singing still."

VIII

Thus spoke the voice, and upon my sight
Sudden the day broke silver white.
"Dawn!" I cried. "It is dawn for me,
And the rising hour of a Day-to-be!"   100
                                                      (1918)

The Fighting Men of Canada

I

There's a moving on the water where the ships have lain asleep,
    There's a rising of the wind along the shore;
There's a cloud that's heading landward, ever dark'ning, from the deep,
    There's a murmur where the crowd was mute before.
        And the order's "Come together!"
            And the word is "Down below!
        There'll be forty kinds o' weather
            When the winds begin to blow!"

II

We have counted up our shekels, we have turned our pennies in,
   We have kissed the girls and closed the waiting line;   10
For there's business over yonder, dirty business for our kin,
   And we're shipping out together on the brine.
     And the call is "Do your duty!
      Bon voyage! Farewell! Adieu!
     There'll be time for love and beauty
      When you've seen the business through!"

III

There's a hush along the river where the tide goes out to sea,
   And a song that echoes softly to the shore,
For the boats have set to seaward, creeping downward in the lee,
   And a grim old dog of war leads on before.   20
     And we sing a song of seamen
      As we pass the answering hill,
     "We are Britons, we are freemen,
      And we'll live as freemen still!"

IV

Myriad-mouthed they hail our coming, break in thunders of applause,
   'Tis the Lion Mother's welcome to her brood!
They have found us worthy kinsmen, bred to serve a worthy cause,
   Men of British nerve and born of British blood.
     But the Captain's eye is leering,
      And the word is "Do your bit!   30
     There'll be time enough for cheering
      When the guns begin to spit!"

V

God, the long mad days of waiting, eating dust and spitting blood,
   While the bullets rake the trenches where we lie!
Curse the hours that hold us steady! Damn the Captain's sober mood,
   Let us run the fiends to hell or let us die!

But the Captain's word is given,
   "Hold the line—we're one to ten!
What's it matter—hell or heaven—
   So we die like fighting men?"   40

VI

Call it lust or call it honour—call it glory in a name!
  We're a handful, more or less, of what we were;
But we praise the great Almighty that we stuck and played the game
  Till we chased them at the double to their lair!
    For the word came, "Up and over!"
      And our answer was a yell
    As we scrambled out of cover—
      And we dealt the dastards hell!

                     (1918)

Good-Byes, a la Mode

I

Mistress A and Mistress B
Toyed with little cups of tea,
Whispered little things they heard
So-and-So say—word for word;
Blackened, every time they spoke,
Names of fairly decent folk;
Spread the scandal You-know-who
Told of Madame Well-to-do;
Who was straight, and who was not—
And more of such damned silly rot!   10
Then they lingered near the door,
Kissed a dozen times or more,
Sang "So long!" and Mistress A
Lied once yet—and went her way!

II

Juliet and Romeo
(Not the two that, long ago,
Mister Shakespeare wrote about)
Sat and watched the tide go out;
Watched the moon above the sea—
Sighed and lied most soulfully;   20
Wished they might for evermore
Sit upon that same old shore;
Held warm hands and kissed a bit—
But what's the use of telling it!
Long each clung to each when they
Sobbed their good-byes, R and J;
Each gave pledge in solemn vow—
Thought they meant it anyhow!

III

Private X and Sapper Y
Met once just to say good-bye;   30
From away back they had stood
Side by side as old pals should;
Now that X was called away,
Both had, oh, so much to say—
Never said a word of it!
They cussed a bit—and swore a bit—
And shook a bit—but spoke no word—
Then X wheeled quick and jumped on board!
Someone placed a credit then
To the names of these two men,   40
Wrote it in the Book above—
"X and Y—two men who love!"

(1918)

The Men Who Stood

WHY, with the odds ten to one, did they stay,
Playing the game for a wager of blood,
Holding a legion of demons at bay
For a day and a night, for a night and a day—
Do you ask why they stood?

Shed on the soul of a man of the plains
Beams of a sun with a quickening ray,
Fill the young blood of his wild coursing veins
Full of the pride of his orient day;
Trace on his brow in the light of the morn   10
Symbols of dreams of a nation to be,
Touch him to visions of cities unborn
Crowding the shores of a shimmering sea;

Bring to the soul of a man of the hills
Harrowing winds from the canyons of snow,
Give him to know in the thing that he wills
Men can be gods though they suffer below;
Show him the stars where they set on the rim
Crowning the granite that lifts to the blue,
Tune the great chords of his soul to the hymn   20
Sung by the planets the living night through;

Give to the soul of a man of the north
Faith in the blood of an unwithered race,
Joy in the labour of infinite worth,
Vigour that grows to an exquisite grace;
Breathe on him tales of his grim-visaged sires,
Teach him the curse of a kingdom in thrall,
Fill him with hate for a nation of liars,
Quicken his heart with a clarion's call;

Then, with the odds ten to one, bid him stay,   30
Face the hell-horrors or welter in blood,
Holding the line with the legions at bay,
And he'll die in his night or he'll live in his day,
But they'll know that he stood!

                                                    (1918)

The Monument

She stood in a city square;
Haggard she was, and worn and pale,
A thing of pity who once was fair;
Weeping about her, her children stood,
Voicing their wants in mournful wail—
Fatherless, homeless, starveling brood!

Above her an image of stone,
Stolid and chill, with rayless eyes
Looked down on the woman wan and lone—
Symbol of honour and vaunted deed   10
Such as a king triumphant buys,
Paying his price in hearts that bleed!

A poet who saw the two from afar
Looked and passed and wondered alone
Which was the symbol of savage war—
Woman and brood, or image of stone!

                                                    (1918)

Albert William Drummond
(b.1887)

—————◆—————

Albert William Drummond was born in Scotland, but joined the Canadian Expeditionary Force (CEF) in 1916 after moving to Halifax. Perhaps the best way to understand Drummond's poetry is to compare it to the work of fellow Scottish immigrant, Robert Service. Like Service, Drummond worked as a stretcher-bearer and, also like Service, his poetry is a strange mix of patriotic celebration of the Empire's struggles and victories and frustration with the devastating human price of war. More than half a decade later, that complicated understanding remained. "War, the curse of humanity, that brings tragedy and sorrow," he wrote about a memorial erected in his newfound home of Guelph, "also brings the spirit of courage, service and sacrifice."[1]

The Battlefield

I stood one day amid the dead,
 'Twas on a battle plain
Somewhere in France, on No Man's Land,
 Forget it I would fain.[2]
But ah! the poignant memory hangs
 Forbidding o'er my soul,
For death was present everywhere,
 Red blood the battle toll.

I saw the dewy earth, God's own,
 Created by His might,   10

---

[1] Albert William Drummond, *Guelph: The Royal City* (Guelph, 1924), 24.
[2] rejoice

Churned up in heaps and twisted mounds,
    Could I forget the sight!
The stench of death was in the air,
    For dead lay all around—
Grotesque and awesome in their sleep—
    Half buried in the ground.

I stepped so warily along,
    Lest by mischance I tread
Upon some shrunken scalp or skull,
    Alone amid the dead.   20
The cold wind rustled as it swept,
    I felt its icy breach,
I neared it whisper as it flew,
    To me it whispered death.

A deadly faintness seized my soul,
    I tried to throw aside,
Where'er I gazed lay ghastly sights,
    All scattered far and wide.
A clenched fist from earthy mound,
A grinning skull close by,   30
The noblest work of God lay still
    With gaping sightless eye.

I saw corruption everywhere,
    I gazed on bloated face,
The yielding body of a man
    Amid this bloody maze—
A man that once did laugh and love,
    Yea! live the same as I.
Now lay legs crossed with arms wide flung,
    Dead, staring to the sky.   40

Some lay alone to stark and stiff,
    Struck down in manhood's flush,

While here and there a motley crowd
    Had fallen in that rush.
One lay alone amid the mud,
    A mangled form and dead,
A letter clutched with icy hand,
    "My darling wife,"—I read.

But was that all? No! charred and burned—
    His rifle by his side—   50
Lay one who'd made the sacrifice,
    Lay one who'd nobly died.
Had died a sacrifice that we
    Serene in peace might dwell,
God! could I e'er forget that sight—
    Forget that awful hell.

Let all who live go swear by God
    That ne'er again shall man
Go forth to war, intent to shed
    Blood of his fellow-man.   60
Let not that blood be on our souls,
    Let war for ever cease,
That man to man the whole world o'er.
    May brothers live in peace.

Say not our loved ones died in vain
    Upon that battle plain,
They died that we might live, achieve
    That prize they sought to gain.
A noble purpose spurred them on,
    To dare, to do, to die,   70
The greatest monument to build,
    World-peace, the strongest tie.

                                                (1918)

The Colonial's Challenge

We have heard the call of the battle
    From a land across the sea,
That dear old land of our fathers,
    The land of the true and free.
We have crossed the sea by the thousand,
    To fight 'neath the Union Jack.
We have promised to do our utmost—
    To conquer or ne'er go back.

We fight and we die in the trenches.
    We drown 'mid the North Sea's roll.   10
By fever, frost, and tempest,
    And reck not of the toll.
We heard the call of our Empire,
    We face the fire and steel,
For a land laid low by a tyrant foe
    To save from the "iron heel."

We have reckoned the cost in the dimness
    That came with the battle's haze,
As we prayed and longed for the homeland
    And for England's primrose ways.   20
But we set our hand with a promise,
    An oath that we ne'er could break.
And the call came loud as thunder,
    These were the words it spake:—

"To my sons, who have crossed the ocean,
    "My whelps of the bulldog breed,
"Your freedom, your birthright is challenged,
    "Come forth! 'tis my hour of need."
We heard, we came at the bidding,
    We answered the call of the blood,   30

But not for the law of Empire
   But to save by the help of God.

To save a nation downtrodden.
   Our honour—that was our bond,
And we ne'er shall cease from the struggle
   'Till we know that by blood they atoned.
Then in that day of our reck'ning,
   When the nations they crushed shall be free,
With vengeance and just retribution,
   For innocents lost in the sea.   40

'Tis not for the love of battle
   We throw our young lives away,
And not for the cause of conquest,
   But for land once free—but to-day
Despoiled, yea, ravished and bleeding
   'Neath the might of a Nero's hand.
God! How can thou e'er misjudge our cause?
   Why, that babe awash on the strand
Looks up to our face, cries vengeance
   Eyes staring, but the stain—   50
It crimsons the locks and that forehead.
   Were their lives to be taken in vain?

                            (1918)

The Empire

What hast thou done, great Empire,
That bound thy sons to thee?
From North, from South, from East and West,
From lands far o'er the sea,
They rallied at thy bidding,
But not for thee alone,
But for ravaged lands despoiled by sword.

Did they make proud might atone.
Deeds hast thou done, great Empire,
And we blush to tell the tale;   10
Deeds hast thou done, great Empire,
And with pride our bosoms swell.
The noblest deed of the ages,
Record in years to be,
That thou drew thy sword for a land laid low,
And to set a people free.

(1918)

On the Banks of the Somme[3]

Come, gather around friend! A story I'll tell.
Yes, a story of action of shot and of shell—
Well, it happened out yonder, I shudder to think
How near I came, lads, to go over the brink.

We were lying entrenched, knee-deep in the mire.
My God! how we suffered from gas and from fire!
Each morning and night we stared death in the face,
But boys, believe me, we set him the pace.

The message from Headquarters came up the line
It said to be ready, all to be steady.   10
Fritz's[4] big guns were making things hum,
Over there, boys—on the banks of the Somme.

---

[3] The Battle of Somme (located near the Somme River in France) took place in 1916. It was a
devastating battle with a high number of losses and minor victories.
[4] A nickname for the Germans during World War I.

The message was read, and our faces grew grim.
I nudges my pal, my pal's name was Jim.
Zero, hour, it was set for six-thirty a.m.
Yes, that was the time, boys, we gave it to them.

Exactly at five the bombardment began.
Slow and continuous, then hurricane.
Machine guns did crackle and rifles did bark,
On the banks of the Somme 'twixt the daylight and dark.   20

We looked at each other, and some of us swore,
But you could not hear it because of the roar;
Fritz shelled us on right, then shifted to left,
The ground all around us was torn and cleft.

Yes we conversed. 'Twas something like this—
"Did Joe get a letter from little Miss?"
"Leave next week"—"My God! That was near."
"If Fritzie continues he'll get us in here."

Then Zero hour came, lads, we over the brink,
We charged o'er that open before you could wink.   30
We gained our objective, and held it that day,
For the blood that was split old Fritzie did pay.

But what was the cost?
Well now, boys, I think—
Blood was the cost—
Ain't it time for a drink?

                                                          (1918)

The Stretcher-Bearers

Bloody 'tis, the work we do,
    But we do it well;

Staggering out o'er No Man's Land,
   Some will never tell
How they cheered a wounded pal
   Hovering near the brink,
Eased his pain and cheered him there,
   Only with a drink.

Bloody 'tis, the work we do,
   But we do it well,   10
Snatching back some poor doomed soul,
   From the brink of hell.
Lift him up so tenderly,
   Carry him with care,
Hear him groan and murmur, lad,
   'Tis his mother's prayer.

Bloody 'tis, the work we do,
   But we do it well,
Gathering up the fragments left,
   Torn by shot and shell.   20
Ease that crimson bandage, lad,
   Ah! he suffers pain!
Some mother's son—he's only one
   Among the many slain.

Bloody 'tis, the work we've done,
   Have we done it well?
Have we done our duty there
   'Mid the shot and shell?
Did we ever stop to think,
   With no weapon near,   30
When we stood defenceless—say,
   Did we ever fear?

                             (1918)

Bernard Freeman Trotter
(1890–1917)

Before travelling to France to fight in the war, Bernard Freeman Trotter had already seen a good bit of North America. He was born in Toronto, Ontario; raised in Wolfville, Nova Scotia; studied in Hamilton, Ontario; and travelled in California—and a good number of these locales show up in his volume of poetry, *A Canadian Twilight and Other Poems of War and Peace* (1917). Ill-health kept Trotter from enlisting in the Canadian Forces; he applied but was rejected. Disappointed but undeterred, Trotter eventually saw action at the front with the British Army. He was killed in action, reportedly by a shell at the end of a long day's work. *Canadian Twilight* was published posthumously.

The poems collected here cover the span of Trotter's journey to war and tell a story of enthusiasm, reluctance, anxiety, and relief. Not surprisingly, Service's *Rhymes of a Red Cross Man* was one of Trotter's favourite books. It is, Trotter writes, "worth reading and re-reading. He gives you modern war with is glamour (for it has glamour in spite of what most of us say), and he gives you it without. You won't read many pages with dry eyes, and yet it doesn't make you morbid or pessimistic."[1] One can say the same about Trotter's own poetry.

A Canadian Twilight

Peace ... Peace ... the peace of dusky shores
And tremulous waters where dark shadows lie;
The stillness of low sounds ... the ripple's urge
Along the keel, the distant thrush's call,
The drip of oars; the calm of dew-filled air;
The peace of afterglow; the golden peace
Of the moon's finger laid across the flood.

Yet ah! how few brief, fleeting moments since,
That same still finger lay at Langemarck,[2]
And touched the silent dead, and wanly moved   10
Across the murky fields and battle lines
Where late my Country's bravest kept their faith.

O heavenly beauty of our northern wild,
I held it once the perfect death to die
In such a scene, in such an hour, and pass
From glory unto glory—Time, perhaps,
May yet retrieve that vision—oh! but now
These quiet hills oppress me: I am hedged
As in that selfish Eden of the dawn
Wherein man fell to rise; and I have sucked   20
The bitter fruit of knowledge,[3] and am robbed
Of my rose-decked contentment, when I hear

---

[1]   Quoted in W.S.W. McLay, introduction to *A Canadian Twilight and Other Poems of War and Peace*, by Bernard Freeman Trotter (Toronto: McClelland, Goodchild & Stewart, 1917), 21–22.

[2]   Sometimes known as the Second Battle of Ypres, the battle at Langemarck took place in late April 1915 and was the first occasion that the Germans used gas on Canadian troops.

[3]   Cf. Genesis 3:1–7.

Though far, the clash of arms, the shouts, the groans—
A world in torment, dying to be saved.

Oh God! the blood of Outram[4] in these veins
Cries shame upon the doom that dams it here
In useless impotence, while the red torrent runs
In glorious spate for Liberty and Right!
Oh, to have died that day at Langemarck!
In one fierce moment to have paid it all—   30
The debt of life to Earth, and Hell, and Heaven!
To have perished nobly in a noble cause!
Untarnished, unpolluted, undismayed,
By the dank world's corruption, to have passed,
A flaming beacon-light to gods and men!
For in the years to come it shall be told
How these laid down their lives, not for their homes,
Their orchards, fields and cities: "They were driven
To slaughter by no tyrant's lust for power;
Of their free manhood's choice they crossed the sea   40
To save a stricken people from its foe.
They died for Justice—Justice owes them this:
That what they died for be not overthrown."

Peace … Peace … not thus may I find peace:
Like a caged leopard chafing at its bars
In ineffectual movement, this clogged spirit
Must pad its life out, an unwilling drone,
In safety and in comfort; at the best
Achieving patience in the gods' despite
And at the worst—somehow the debt is paid.   50

Lake Cecebe,[5] June 1915.
    (*Written while frail health prevented enlistment.*)
                                            (1917)

---

[4]   Sir James Outram (1803–1863); a British general and military hero.
[5]   Lake in central Ontario, north of Huntsville.

Dreams

Not as we dream them,
    Rose-sweet and wonderful,
Laughter-thrilled, magical,
    Our dreams come true.

Always some hidden,
    Unforeseen circumstance,
Seeming malevolence,
    Darkens the view.

Something we want not,
    Ugly and masterful,   10
Sprouts through the beautiful,
    Wars with our joy.

Someone is missing:
    Gone the sweet comradeship,
Commerce of eye and lip—
    Barren is Troy.[6]

Yet go we ever,
    Though earthly experience
Mocks at their radiance,
    Dreaming our dreams.   20

Dreams without reason,
    Rose-sweet and wonderful,
Laughter-thrilled, magical.—
    Fools?—So it seems.

---

[6] The Trojan war was won when the Trojans accepted a large gift that, unknown to them,
contained the soldiers who would slaughter them in their sleep (Greek mythology).

Or is there a feeble
　　Spark of the infinite
Burning in Hell's despite,
　　In me and you,

Lighting us onward
　　Through the inscrutable   30
To a land wonderful
Where, as we dream them,
　　Our dreams will come true?

Toronto, March 1916.
(Written on the eve of his departure for England.)

(1917)

"*Ici Repose*"[7]

A little cross of weather-silvered wood,
Hung with a garish wreath of tinselled wire,
And on it carved a legend—thus it runs:
"*Ici repose*—" Add what name you will,
And multiply by thousands: in the fields,
Along the roads, beneath the trees—one here,
A dozen there, to each its simple tale
Of one more jewel threaded star-like on
The sacrificial rosary of France.

And as I read and read again those words,   10
Those simple words, they took a mystic sense;
And from the glamour of an alien tongue
They wove insistent music in my brain,
Which, in a twilight hour, when all the guns
Were silent, shaped itself to song.

---

[7]　"Here lies" (French).

O happy dead! who sleep embalmed in glory,
  Safe from corruption, purified by fire,—
Ask you our pity?—ours, mud-grimed and gory,
  Who still must grimly strive, grimly desire?

You have outrun the reach of our endeavour,   20
  Have flown beyond our most exalted quest,—
Who prate of Faith and Freedom, knowing ever
That all we really fight for's just—a rest,

The rest that only Victory can bring us—
  Or Death, which throws us brother-like by you—
The civil commonplace in which 'twill fling us
  To neutralize our then too martial hue.

But you have rest from every tribulation
  Even in the midst of war; you sleep serene,
Pinnacled on the sorrow of a nation,   30
In cerements⁸ of sacrificial sheen.

Oblivion cannot claim you: our heroic
  War-lustred moment, as our youth, will pass
To swell the dusty hoard of Time the Stoic,
  That gathers cobwebs in the nether glass.⁹

We shall grow old, and tainted with the rotten
  Effluvia of the peace we fought to win,
The bright deeds of our youth will be forgotten,
  Effaced by later failure, sloth, or sin;

---

⁸ clothing for the grave
⁹ Bottom half of an hourglass; the hourglass is often associated with allegorical figures of death
   or time.

But you have conquered Time, and sleep forever,   40
*   Like gods, with a white halo on your brows—*
Your souls our lode-stars, your death-crowned endeavour
*   The spur that holds the nations to their vows.*

France, April 1917.
(His last poem, the manuscript of which reached his parents the day
after he was killed.)

(1917)

The Poplars

O, a lush green English meadow—it's there that I would lie—
A skylark singing overhead, scarce present to the eye,
And a row of wind-blown poplars against an English sky.

The elm is aspiration, and death is in the yew,[10]
And beauty dwells in every tree from Lapland to Peru;
But there's magic in the poplars when the wind goes through.

When the wind goes through the poplars and blows them silver white,
The wonder of the universe is flashed before my sight:
I see immortal visions: I know a god's delight.

I catch the secret rhythm that steals along the earth,   10
That swells the bud, and splits the burr, and gives the oak its girth,
That mocks the blight and canker with its eternal birth.

It wakes in me the savor of old forgotten things,
Before "reality" had marred the child's imaginings:
I can believe in fairies—I see their shimmering wings.

---

[10]   species of tree

I see with the clear vision of that untainted prime,
Before the fool's bells jangled in and Elfland ceased to chime,
That sin and pain and sorrow are but a pantomime—

A dance of leaves in ether, of leaves threadbare and sere,[11]
From whose decaying husks at last what glory shall appear   20
When the white winter angel leads in the happier year.

And so I sing the poplars; and when I come to die
I will not look for jasper walls, but cast about my eye
For a row of wind-blown poplars against an English sky.

Oxford, September 1916.

(1917)

---

[11] dry

Frank Prewett

(1893–1962)

After growing up in rural south-western Ontario, Frank Prewett studied at the University of Toronto until war broke out in Europe. Inspired by feelings of national duty, he enlisted as a member of the Eaton Machine Gun Brigade and was later transferred to Royal Field Artillery. Like so many of his fellow soldiers who saw action at the front, Prewett's experience in the war was particularly damaging. At first, Prewett saw the war as a chance to prove Canada's greatness and independence; later, he would see it in less flattering terms. In a letter to his confidante, Lady Ottoline Morrell, he could only defend his strange and erratic postwar behaviour as a consequence of his war injuries.[1] The injuries mentioned only briefly in that letter had earned

---

[1] Frank Prewett to Lady Ottoline Morrell, 10 August 1919. Lady Ottoline Violet Anne Cavendish-Bentinck Morrell Collection, Harry Ransom Center, University of Texas, Austin.

Prewett a release from the war, a stint in the Craiglockhart war hospital, treatment by the famous W.H.R. Rivers, and a chance meeting with Siegfried Sassoon, who became a travelling companion and mentor. Prewett returned to England in 1921 and served again during the Second World War.

Although Prewett garnered praise from the modernist Virginia Woolf, his reputation has rested on his status as a Georgian poet. Included by Edward Marsh in the wildly popular *Georgian Poetry* series, Prewett was, for a long time, known only as a Georgian poet, combining a modern interest in realism and individualism with a neo-romantic nostalgia for pastoral scenes and spiritual uplift. Prewett's *The Rural Scene* (1924) is almost stereotypically Georgian and focuses largely on the certainties and comforts of woodlands and birdsongs. His war poems are less obviously committed to the Georgian mode.

Burial Stones

The blue sky arches wide
From hill to hill;
The little grasses stand
Upright and still.

Only these stones to tell
The deadly strife,
The all-important schemes,
The greed for life.

For they are gone, who fought;
But still the skies   10
Stretch blue, aloof, unchanged,
From rise to rise.

(1921)

Card Game

Hearing the whine and crash
We hastened out
And found a few poor men
Lying about.

I put my hand in the breast
Of the first met.
His heart thumped, stopped, and I drew
My hand out wet.

Another, he seemed a boy,
Rolled in the mud   10
Screaming, "my legs, my legs,"
And he poured out his blood.

We bandaged the rest
And went in,
And started again at our cards
Where we had been.

(1987)

The Soldier

My years I counted twenty-one
Mostly at tail of plough:
The furrow that I drove is done,
To sleep in furrow now.

I leapt from living to the dead
A bullet was my bane.
It split this nutshell rind of head,
This kernel of a brain.

A lad to life has paid his debts
Who bests and kills his foe,   10
And man upon his sweetheart gets,
To reap as well as sow.

But I shall take no son by hand,
No grey beard bravo be:
My ghost is tethered in the sand
Afar from my degree.

(1987)

Soliloquy

To sleep, to die and sleep,
Always to lie abed[2]
By the side of the road;
What peace for this head

To have no dread at night,
No thirst, no hungry need,
No vainly fluttering hands;
God, that were bliss indeed.

Oh fain would I be there
At the side of the road,   10
Were I but sure the mind
Escapes the flesh abode.

But the guts rot, the skin breaks,
The jaws grin, the eyes sink:
Not that, or not that! I faint
With loathing if I think.

(1987)

---

2   Cf. *Hamlet*, 3.2.66–67.

The Survivor

What this reptile worm or snake
Creeps on its torpid scales, creeps
Winding and lengthening its wake
While God above it sleeps

Tempest crushes it, wind assails:
On its bayonets gleam
Lightnings, yet it prevails
And filters through valley and stream

A thousand men to make a beast
Than beast more cumbered each: 10
Sodden and splintered to the feast,
The muddied feast of death they reach

We are mad after thirty years
We who live are mad in the peace.
I left my life there, kept its fears:
From the regiment is no release

While the shells crashed we were strong
Grenade and sniper we defied:
Now I am old, stay overlong
For in those many men I died   20
                                                   (1987)

A.J.M. Smith
(1902–1980)

As a poet, critic, and anthologist, A.J.M. Smith was one of Canadian modernism's first practitioners and most passionate advocates. Born in Westmount and educated at McGill University, Smith and fellow students F.R. Scott (son of Frederick George Scott) and Leon Edel started the influential and groundbreaking *The McGill Fortnightly Review*—just one in a long list of editorial and critical projects that urged Canadian poets to leave behind the trappings of an older, more traditional poetry and embrace the energies and innovations of the new.

Smith's most anthologized poem, "The Lonely Land" (1926), is likely his tribute to the Group of Seven; but, as Brian Trehearne's *A.J.M. Smith: The Complete Poems* (2007) makes obvious, he wrote on a variety of subjects, from jazz to Greek mythology to politics to war. Smith talked about "A Soldier's Ghost" as a warning to future generations who may not remember the costs of past wars. The hallmarks of a loose, imagist form is here, but so too is the influence of Rupert Brooke in the poem's obscure closing images.

A Soldier's Ghost

How shall I speak
To the regiment of young
Whose throats break
Saluting the god

Descending onto the drumhead
—Stalled
Each in his proper stance
Upholding the service?

Bones
Distilled in the frontier sand   10
Fumble
The natty chevron.[1]

Can a memberless ghost
Tell?
These lost
Are so many brother bones.

The hieroglyph
Of ash
Concedes an anagram
Of love.   20
                                    (1934)

---

[1] badge, sometimes indicating length of service

Appendix A: Canadian Authors Writing about World War I

The selections that follow offer a wide range of interpretations about the war, demonstrating that it did not have a single and stable meaning—even for the men who fought in it. The following interpretations include Frank Prewett's suggestion that the war is an opportunity to realize national strength and independence; Peregrine Acland's argument that war is a necessary and noble pursuit; Robert Service's recognition of war's frustrations, injuries, and obscurities; and John Daniel Logan's understanding of war as a chance to remember the dead and be reminded of a spiritual life.

Frank Prewett, Letter to James Mavor, 11 February 1915. From the James Mavor Collection, Thomas Fisher Rare Book Library, University of Toronto.

19 Grenadier Road,
Toronto, February 11, 1915

Prof. James Mavor,
Department of Economics

Dear Sir:—

I am sending this letter in answer to your request that all who enlist for active service should notify you of the circumstances. Chiefly it has been a feeling of injured pride that has drawn me into the force. I have felt hurt to see that those very men who are Canadians, if there can be said to be a Canadian nationality yet, men who have received all the advantages and none of the hardships of this country, are yet the men who are remaining at home and permitting those who have a less careful physical and mental development to represent their country in this great war that is changing the whole life of the world, and which in its change is going to determine to the eyes of all nations whether this Canada of ours is a colony or a great and distinct people independent and confident in thought, feeling and action.

I receive [sic] my uniform to-day, and will take my place in the Eaton gun battery.

Yours truly,

Frank Prewett.

Frank Prewett, Letter to Lady Ottoline Morrell, 10 August 1919. From the Lady Ottoline Violet Anne Cavendish-Bentinck Morrell Collection. Harry Ransom Center, University of Texas in Austin.

Moult,
Salcombe,
S. Devon
10/8/19

Dear Lady Ottoline—[1]

I am sorry that I was the unfortunate cause of disappointment to you. When you put a sting into every line of your letter you are merely adding to the recrimination which, for years, I have myself cherished against my own physical incapability and my deficiency of normal manly instincts. I hope you are not so disillusioned that you wish to cease to know me. I cannot express myself in words; as you know, words are not the means but the obstacles to expression. I feel only too keenly that my actions are all gauche. For all that, let us be friends, not perfunctory acquaintances. If I say that you have brought great happiness to me, widened my vision, and made me unselfconscious, you will retort "kind Lady Ottoline and Visitor's Book," yet you know in your heart that my feeling towards you has never for one

---

[1] Lady Morrell was a well-connected figure in English society. After staying with Morrell at her estate, Prewett returned to Ontario and continued to write to her, discussing literature, the war, and his ill-health.

moment inclined to any such spaniel unpleasantness. As far as I am concerned, you are my dear friend, and no change of attitude upon your part can change me, though it might compel a change in the obvious things. Please let me know that this present disappointed unfamiliarity which you feel towards me is past and ended. After all, one is conversational with many, and intimate with few, in this world. It is no light thing in my life to forego intimacy.

What I do feel towards humanity I do not know, but I can discover sometimes what I do not feel. I do not love humanity in the active manner that I love individuals. I have no passionate feeling towards them. One time, perhaps, I might have been passionate, but the war made me old, body and mind, and, unfortunately, while my mind has had sufficient elasticity to recover its youth, my body has not. When you condemn me, do not forget this thing. I move about the world in a maze, an uncomprehended vagueness. I see the eagerness of life, but I feel none of it. It is so hazardous, so short, so mysterious, so ironic, this life of humanity, that I cannot bring myself to plunge seriously and enthusiastically into it. Occasionally I meet in this uncomprehended vagueness individuals who are sympathetic. What I have, I give freely to these individuals. I would give more if I had more. Do not tell me that we are to become tolerating acquaintances. Do not assume my lack of intensity of feeling.

The blue-and-gold existence knows neither event nor change. I have not left the grounds since my arrival. A day or two I was not well. All these people here oppress me with their aggressive health and strength. They are forever active. What they are thinking, God knows.

Please write, a note if no more, to make my mind less anxious. I feel that I must seem to you to be a cad, and yet I neither am nor have been one.

I hope you are well, and that you have exorcised the demon of head-ache.

Yours,
Frank

John Daniel Logan, "The Fatal Paradox and Sin of Sorrow for the Dead." *Insulters of Death and Other Poems of the Great Departure*. Halifax: L. Clyde Davidson, 1916. 31–36.

The current iniquitous and ruthless war has greatly enlarged the world of Death. The only way to decrease its empire, to reduce it to insignificance, is to enlarge the world of Life. The enlargement of the world of Life is a personal duty for each individual still alive. Once undertaken, it will result in the enhancement and ennobling of existence, and in the discovery of ineffable and compelling consolation for the spirit, not only in spite of the tribulations of existence but also in very virtue of them. The only way to enlarge the world of Life is for each living individual voluntarily to establish, consciously to create, connections with the noumenal,[2] the incorporeal, the invisible, the impalpable world—the world of Spirits Departed.

I am not recommending any species of necromancy, occult science, clairvoyance, clairaudience, or spiritualistic transports. My point of view is human and logical—practicable; my aim is as practical as it is human; and my method of creating connections with the Departed is as sane as it is simple and effectual. [...] [Here, Logan proceeds to offer a lengthy analogy that compares the departure of a new bride from her husband's home to the departure of a soldier from the physical world.]

[...] In some such terms of similitude we should think of death—of the departure of our dead into the noumenal, into the spiritual world. If we individually will thus to think of death, we shall not have suffered loss by the death of those we love, but have gained a three-fold good for our spirits while we sojourn on earth. For the dead have not died—our beloved have not departed—futilely, to no purpose, even for us who remain behind; they have died, departed, *to enlarge the world of life.*

Strange paradox it may seem; but recall our simile of the departed bride and we shall readily see the threefold—nay, more

---

[2]   that which can only be known by the mind

than threefold—gain that death brings us, the living—if we, the living, but *will* the gain to be real and ever present. Gone hence from us into another world, as our dead have gone, they wait upon us to have "other-worldly" thoughts of them, to follow them thither in affectionate memory, and to resuscitate them by spiritual communion with them, not as unreal spectres but as real persons. Sorrow—continued, excessive sorrow—over our dead is an absolute fatality: it prevents the resurrection of our dead: for it implies a belief on our part in a great gulf fixed between the living and the departed, nay, the utter vanishment and irrevocable loss of our beloved. Sorrow is equally fatal to us and to them; it blinds our eyes, so that we no longer behold the dead beckoning to us, importuning us for resuscitation in our minds and hearts; and it drives them away from us into the abyss of nothingness. This is our fault, our sin. But by memory of our dead, spiritual communing with them, we immediately establish a real and abiding connection between this world and the extra-mundane sphere—between earth and Heaven. Surely it is obvious that if there were no death, no departure hence of our beloved, there would be no "other world," no pure and ennobling thoughts of "other-worldliness." We are debtors to our dead—and we can be their homagers;[3] they have opened up and made real and lovely the "other world" of Spirits Departed. How great a gain, then, for us on earth—this tender thinking on death as departure, this communion with our dead, this resurrection of them, which is an enlargement of the world of Life. [...]

Now, this is the fatal paradox and sin of sorrow for the dead. It is not by dying, that is, parting from mundane existence, that our beloved really, absolutely are dead. It is the living who make them dead, either by *sorrow*, which denies their existence in the realm of Spirits Departed, and the possibility of joyous communion with them there; or by *forgetfulness* of them, which is a refusal to resuscitate and resurrect those who have died. Men and women do not

---

[3]   those who pay homage or show respect

absolutely die at the moment of the dissolution of body and spirit. As a cosmological process death is no more significant in human beings than it is in any other animate creatures, animal or vegetable. It is merely dissolution and transmutation. Men and women become dead, *after* they die, by a slow, spiritual process—by our gradual forgetfulness of them, or, as Tom Hood beautifully and truthfully put it, when, as time passes, there comes to be of them

"No resurrection in the minds of men."[4]

The only real and everlasting death is *oblivion*—obliteration of the departed from the thoughts, affectionate memory and converse of the living. For us, the living, to permit continued, excessive sorrow for our beloved dead, or for us to permit oblivion of them, by forgetting them totally, is to be guilty of the most terrible homicide—we utterly slay, not mortal bodies, but pure spirits. To cause such real and enduring death is an unpardonable sin. [...]

(1916)

From Robert Service, *Records of a Red Cross Man*. "R.W. Service Shelled to Shelter, Hides on Hill of a Hundred Horrors." *Toronto Daily Star*, December 11, 1915, 2.[5]

A Sudden Call

[...] "AMBULANCE wanted."

An orderly stands in the doorway, a telegram in his hand. I read it: "Hill 71, three wounded, send car at once." Sadly we leave our untasted luncheon and seek the car.

Singularly dreary is the way to Hill 71. Here in the line of fire there has been no effort to till the land, and the ungathered beets of last year have grown to seed. Amid rank, unkept fields we race over a road

---

[4]   See Thomas Hood's "Sonnet (It is not death, that sometime in a sigh)" (1823).

[5]   Published in a few regional newspapers in Canada, Service's *Records of a Red Cross Man* was a series of weekly correspondent pieces beginning on 11 December 1915 and running until 29 January 1916. *Rhymes of a Red Cross Man* was published later that year. The pieces read as documents of Service's experiences as a stretcher-bearer and ambulance driver, and supplied home front citizens with an intimate portrait of the heroes and horrors of the war.

that is pitted with obus holes. On both sides runs a telephone wire, supported by slim saplings. We pass soldiers returning from the trenches, mud-caked, and ineffably weary. Suddenly, coming over the crest of a hill we see the upward slope of the countryside streaked with grey lines—the trenches.

The German Trenches

"Look yonder, on the ridge of the hill," says the orderly who has come to guide us. "Yon bank of gravel—that's the Boches;[6] that's their first line."

"Why, it looks quite harmless, quite deserted."

"It isn't though. It's alive with the pigs. They can see us quite plainly. No doubt they have their glasses on us even now. Don't linger. We must hurry over this bit of road."

But it is difficult to believe that sun-flecked grey line means danger, and our eyes follow it incredulously. Then we dip down out of sight, and in the hollow we find the dressing station.

A gang of sappers are digging a communication trench. From the doors of their dug-outs the fantassins[7] stare at us. A grey-haired doctor comes from the dressing station that is excavated in the side of the hill.

"I have two men wounded, by a grenade. There is a third, but we want you to wait a little for him. We think he is dying."

The two are lifted into the car. They star dully; they make no sound. From hip to heel one is swathed in bandages. The other has a great white turban on his head, a turban with a red patch that spreads and spreads. They seem to have no pain. Now we must wait for the third.

The Baptism of Fire

And while we wait something happens. There is a shrill, screaming noise. I see sudden fear come into the faces of the stretcher-bearers, but the next moment I am gazing at something else. In a little hollow

---

[6] Germans (slang)
[7] "Infantryman; footsoldier" (French).

some 40 yards away there is an explosion that reminds me of a mine blast; then a sudden belch of coal-black smoke. I stare at it stupidly. It looks fresh, lively, ugly, a very black snake-head of smoke, savage, and hissing. Beside it, all luminous in the sunlight, there is a patch of poppies. That coiling smoke cloud looks deplorably out of place, I think. I resent it intensely; I— Then turning round I find I am alone. Like magic every one has vanished, dived like rabbits into their burrows. Perhaps I too had better do a rabbit act. But no! There are the wounded in the car. It doesn't seem right to leave them. It's a poor time, though, to weigh pros and cons. Ah! happy thought. Never shall it be said that I deserted my car; I'll get under it.

So I crawl beneath the motor, and just as I do so there is a second blood-curdling stream, a second smoke-burst, but this time nearer us by 20 yards. Every shell-scream is an interrogation; the answer— what? According to my calculations the next shell is due to fall plumb on the car, on me, and lying there on my stomach in the mud I reflect sadly on the epics I shall never live to write. But a minute passes; nothing comes. Another minute, still nothing. Then the doctor hails me from his shelter.

"Ah, the Boches will have their little joke. This place is not quite safe. You must not stay here too long."

I agree. It is not exactly the place I would choose for a picnic. I am not lingering just for the fun of the thing. I am waiting for a man to die. (In my heart I believe I wish he'd hurry up and do it.)

Then the doctor: "Ah, yes; you wait for the other. But now I do not think it is worth while. You see, you are drawing their fire. While you stay here it is dangerous for us all. You had better go."

I need no second bidding. Joyfully I crank up and get to highest speed. As if nothing had happened the trench-diggers have resumed their work. As I mount the fatal hill again I cannot help looking back. There, a corrugated line against the sky is the German trench, more silent, more deserted, more innocent-looking than ever.

(1915)

Robert Service, *Records of a Red Cross Man* cont. "At the Field Dressing Station During an Attack." *Ottawa Journal,* January 22, 1916, 2.

The Arrival

By the side of the road, under cover of the bank, are groups of soldiers, blue-coated, recumbent figures, some munching at fistfuls of dry bread, others waiting in an attitude of patient resignation. Many of them are bald-headed, grizzle-bearded, fathers of families, lovers of home and peace. And here they are waiting, waiting to be launched into a very inferno of carnage. No wonder they look at us with eyes of melancholy. No doubt each is thinking: "Perhaps in a few hours one of these very cars will be taking the dripping thing that is left of me away. Perhaps this very bread I am eating will be my last. Perhaps I'll never see that red sun rise again. And yet it isn't of myself I'm thinking."

So I seem to read those sombre faces by the wayside. But now the roar of hidden guns has grown incessant around us, and every moment it becomes more violent. Then as we skirt the shadow of a wood a hospital orderly runs to meet us. He is trembling with excitement.

"You must go no further. Draw up well concealed under the trees and twenty yards apart, and await orders." [...]

The Work Begins

"Hurry up, there. The ambulance is wanted."

A soldier is running to seek me. The other cars have already gone. There is work, lots of it, though the attack is not due till seven. I start up the car and drive forward to the village. There at the poste de secours I get my first cases. They are both unconscious. I am glad of this. Unconscious men don't groan and cry out at the rough places on the road, and the rough places are many, and their cries unnerve one so.

"Take them to the hospital in F.," says the doctor in charge. "Do you know the way?"

"No, but I've a tongue to ask."

As I start a man with his arm bandaged from shoulder to wrist begs me for a lift, so I tell him to climb on the seat beside me. The linen that swathes his arm is blood-soaked, and he nurses it very tenderly, drawing little hissing breaths of pain. He also leans against me as I drive. Then suddenly his eyes close and his weight grows heavy, so I know that he has fainted.

It is no joke driving two unconscious men and supporting a third over a road you don't know, with a car you don't understand. However, Dorthea,[8] realizing her responsibilities, rises to the occasion. Perhaps it is the extra weight, but she goes steadily and well. The road is a fair road, stony, hilly, twisty, but a good road for these parts, and in about half an hour I arrive at F. Now, think I; I will soon get my passengers off my hands. But there is much confusion, and I am directed to three different hospitals before I am relieved.

Back to the Bomb-Belt

Once more with my buggy I make for the bomb-belt. The sky is brazen now, the young day broiling hot. The road, so recently deserted, is suddenly a-seeth with traffic. There are strings of ammunition wagons, food convoys, regiments of the reserve, all moving towards that distant thunder in a cloud of dust. The men walk wearily, and sweat under their heavy coats. They are dirty, unshaven, grim, always grim, though here and there is one who flaunts a ghastly gaiety. [...]

The Dressing-Station

All at once just beside me I hear an explosion that for a moment stuns me. I look in its direction. There in a pit by the side of the road is a great, squat field mortar, and it has thrown a shell clean over the car. I almost imagine anyone standing on top would have been hit. I can see the gunners jump out of their holes after the shot, but I do not stop to analyze my sensations. Instead I speed Dorothea up another notch. Ah! there is the dressing station. It is a long dug-out with two entrances, one to take in the wounded, the other to bring them out. It stands on the flattish top of a rise, but is indistinguishable from the

---

[8]   "Dorothea" is the name that Service gives his ambulance.

clay of the road. Beyond it is a narrow trail, up which a stream of Red Cross men are pushing stretchers mounted on wheels. From where they are coming shells are falling thick and fast, but they do not seem to heed. Already rank on rank of stretchers lie on the ground, limp heaps that go into the dug-out dirty, mangled, bloody, to come out stripped, swathed, straightened, but still bloody.

Never will I forget it, that bright bare field on the hill, the young barley all around, the long road lined with blue-coated soldiers, the guns blazing on all sides; the crash of shells falling in the trenches. The sharp, cool doctor gives his orders, the Red Cross men drip with sweat as they unload their burdens, the half-naked forms on the stretchers quiver in the fierce heat, the blind glare. There is a strange metallic feeling in the air, while spouting geysers of smoke, white, yellow, black, seem to ring us all around.

The Wave of Wounded

I cannot turn the car in that narrow road with the wounded lying under my very wheels, so some soldiers swing it around for me. Then again two mangled heaps are lifted in. One has been wounded by a bursting gun. There seems to be no part of him that is not burned, and I marvel that he lives. The skin of his breast is a blueish color and cracked open in ridges. I am sorry I saw him. After this, when they put the things that once were men into my car I will turn away my head.[9]

Again I make my way to F., but it is more difficult than ever now for the road is fearfully encumbered. The stream of traffic runs both ways. On the one hand there are fresh regiments going out to the slaughter, on the other the wounded pouring back from it. I pass bands of them struggling hospitalwards. Most are hit on the arm or foot, but some have heads bound and faces masked with dried blood. Slowly, wearily they walk, some like somnambulists,[10] starting at the

---

[9] The section "One has been wounded ... turn away my head" was not printed in the *Toronto Star*. P.D. Ross, the editor of the *Ottawa Journal* (which printed the piece in full), was admonished by chief censor Lieutenant-Colonel Ernest J. Chambers for printing the full account.
[10] sleepwalkers

sound of my horn, and having to be dragged out of the way. Often they sink by the roadside, a band of fifty or so, then a Red Cross orderly shouts at them and goads them on a little further. Many throw away their cartridges so that in places the road fairly glitters.

In the car behind me I can hear a man sobbing: "Ah! cette guerre! cette guerre!" and never was [a] cry more full of bitterness and grief. As I draw near my goal his plaints grow more acute. I can feel him gently padding on the canvas at my back, but whether to hurry or go slower, I know not. I only know that the place where he taps is bright with blood. But the longest way has its end, and with intense relief I get rid of my load. I deliver them to a little fat surgeon, whose hands against his white smock are scarlet bright, and I can see other surgeons, other stretchers, each with its bit of mangled flesh and bone.[11] [...]

Dorothea Demurs

On coming out I find Dorothea boiling furiously, and try to cool her with some water I get from a duck pond. I am starting back for the firing line when a Red Cross orderly asks me for a lift. He tells me he knows a shorter way back to the village, so that I can return more quickly. Inwardly I wish he knew of one ten times as long. I would take it joyfully. But after all, things do not turn out so badly, for he gives me a wrong direction, and presently we find ourselves in a narrow cart road amid the open fields.

The question is whether to turn back or go on. We decide that if we go a little further we may strike the main road again. Alas! vain hope. The cart road degenerates into two mere ruts in the clay, and grows momentarily ruttier. Dorothea doesn't like it at all. She bucks several times, and makes alarming noises. Then while I am negotiating a steep bank of clay she suddenly tries to turn a somersault. I don't know whether it is because in the excitement I switch on the gas instead of shutting it off, but after a moment of wild confusion we find ourselves panting in the middle of a mangold[12] field.

---

[11] This entire paragraph is absent in the *Toronto Star* version of "The Attack."
[12] root vegetabale with a leafy top

I am quite content to stay there, quite. I discover an idyllic quality in mangold fields I had not hitherto suspected. There is no sign of life, no sign of strife, just peace and rest and quietness. Willingly would I have lurked there till dewy eve, then crawled virtuously home, but alas! there is the Red Cross man to recall me to my sense of duty. Yes, the bomb-belt again for me. Sadly and with difficulty I detach Dorothea from the mangolds, and coax her back once more to the straight and stony path.

(1916)

Robert Service, *Records of a Red Cross Man* cont. "The Valley of a Thousand Dead." *Toronto Daily Star*, January 8, 1916, 4.

The Grave-Seekers

[...] [T]hey are all alike, these French officers, overwhelming in their kindness and courtesy. A few weeks ago one of them offered to accompany me to a nearby village that has its quotidian bombardment. My object was to find if a certain soldier was buried there.

The day was crammed with sunshine; the fields bright with young wheat. In places there was a wonderful flame of poppies, and the larks were singing all down the sky. Never could you imagine a scene more brimful of peace and joy. And yet ever we heard the grumble of distant guns, and above the grey, snaking lines of the German trenches we could see puffs of smoke start and hover. Our artillery was firing well.

Then there was another distraction. An aeroplane appeared in the serene blue, which instantly began to form in bursting shrapnel. The rapid-firers, too, throbbed and purred, and the air was full of action. We were right in the line of the shooting. I could see the captain was fidgety, and this surprised me, the more so as he wore the cross of bravery in the field.

Courage of the Captain

"Perhaps it seems to you," he said, looking anxiously heavenward. "As if I lack courage?"

Not at all. Courage is, after all, too often only a lack of the danger sense."

"It's true, anyway, I do lack courage. I confess it. I will give you an instance, my friend. It was in those hellish days of the great retreat. My regiment was fighting a rear-guard action, and my colonel gave me a despatch for the general. Part of my way lay across some mud flats, which simply sprayed by the Boche fire. When I came to this place, I admit it, my legs seemed to turn to jelly. I fell flat on the mud. I was horribly afraid. I felt I could go no further. But there was my despatch. I must deliver that. So I commenced to creep forward, taking every bit of cover. I could not get close enough to that mud. For over two miles I crawled on my stomach through the vile mire. I summoned my will-power, cursed myself, called myself ugly names, but rise I could not. However, I got to headquarters and delivered my despatch."

The captain with the military medal squinted with some relief up at that blue sky in which the Taube[13] was fast disappearing.

"Well, on the way back the general gave me an orderly to accompany me. This made all the difference. We came to the mud flats, still raked by that deadly fire. I felt just as afraid, but there was no hesitation, no wavering now. Why? Because this soldier was with me, had his eyes upon me, respected me. I must at least make a bluff at bravery. So I drew myself up; I marched erect; I smiled gaily. I expected every moment would be my last, but I did not show it. I do not know what his feelings were. He followed me, though, marching erect. I laughed contemptuously at that rain of fire. I lit a cigaret. I joked. And all the time I wanted to sink into the ground, to crawl, to grovel. Well, we got over the dangerous place without mishap. My reputation for coolness was made. I got the cross. But do you think I am proud of it? No; I admit I have no courage." [...]

(1916)

---

13   A kind of airplane used by the Germans.

Peregrine Acland, "Thoughts of a Returned Soldier." *The Rebel* 2.3, December 1917, 97–101.[14]

Was it worth while—to plunge into the sulphurous depths of hell and clamber out on the far side of the pit's rim, for what? To potter through fifty years of life in the suburbs or to toil for half a century in the slums? These are the questions that hundreds of thousands of returned men, in all the belligerent countries, are beginning to ask themselves, and which will soon be felt, if not uttered, by millions of the world's youth, German as well as British, Austrian as well as French. For they have seen war and have seen that it was terrible, and yet have discovered that the hardships and bitter sufferings of open strife were not so appalling as the monotony and miseries that so frequently beset that life of peace in which the body found safety and the soul too often found death.

Never before perhaps has so large a proportion of the youth of the world taken part in a combat for a cause which they knew to be great. Fighting was for centuries the privilege and the pleasure of the classes. It has now become the obligation—and the privilege, too—of the masses. Picture to yourself those hundreds of thousands of workers in many lands, by many seas, busy at their tens of thousands of occupations, of trade, of business, of science and of art, in which they laboured for their own well-being and advantage, with little thought of the great world—then suddenly plucked away by the claws of Fate and hurled into this vast conflict of the nations. Think of their astonishment! Life has suddenly become for them a matter of infinite wonder, whose very terrors have enhanced its beauties. They are no longer left to their own small purpose, but are suddenly placed under the direction of a great aim to which they must render the utmost

---

[14] Acland (1891–1963) served in the war with the 48th Highlanders and was wounded at Thiepval in September 1916. Aside from his military contributions, Acland is best known for his *All Else Is Folly* (1929), a novel that writer Ford Madox Ford calls an account of a "soul's sufferings" and scholar Jonathan F. Vance labels "antiwar" and "modernist." This address strikes a decidedly different note and was delivered before the Women's Canadian Club at Ottawa on 5 October 1917.

service of their ability. It is rudely demanded of them that they live heroically, venture their all upon a game with Fate, seek death that they may overcome it. This is as if, having been dwellers on the plain, they suddenly find themselves struggling towards the mountain-tops.

When the war is over, are they to go back to the old, hard, dull, meaningless existence upon the plain? But, it will be said, we cannot always live upon the mountain-tops of life. No? Yet at least we can always live within sight of them. And this war will be of little use, it will not have been worth the cost in blood and agony, unless mankind remembers that a life that is not dominated and inspired by a great aim and illumined by spiritual grandeur is infinitely worse than death upon the field. [...]

Are danger and strife then so splendid, so necessary, to give a background of magnificence to our lives? Yes, and the greater the danger, the keener the strife, the more superb is the reward. To fight in a good cause is the best, but to fight well in any cause that seems good is as much as can be expected of man. To fight is to live. The real objection to war is that there is so little fighting in it. Months of weary waiting, long spells of enforced inactivity in which the mind sickens with disgust at a wasted life, followed by as long spells of heart-breaking and back-breaking gigantic labours in the mud and darkness, then one fiery charge of half an hour, and three-quarters of those who rushed into the melee are out of the combat, crippled or silent, resting on the breast of their earth-mother.

What must we do, then, if we would have war shed its splendours over a greater portion of our lives? Establish it on a limited liabilities basis, go back to some form of fighting involving less sudden whole-sale slaughter? No, we must abolish war entirely on the physical plane as being the most sordid, the most uninteresting, the most expensive, and the least satisfactory of all forms of combat. We must make the world safe—which is to say we must keep the ring—for that spiritual and intellectual strife which is the noblest of all forms of the gladiatorial struggle.

All life must be our field of battle, a field on which the first, the most difficult and the most constantly to be repeated triumph must be that over our own indifference, slothfulness and cowardice, and the second and probably less generally welcomed attack must be upon the similar indifference, slothfulness and cowardice of our friends.[15] We are not only all sinners, we are all cowards. But we must put aside that timidity if we would live fully, and must take courage to dare to live finely and intensely. It takes no less degree of valour to assail a social injustice or to challenge an established hypocrisy than to go over the parapet. And it requires no less coolness of head here than in Flanders to save ourselves from wasting time and strength in injudicious attacks at the wrong points, and so to lay our plans that we may be able to strike at the right place at the right moment, and strike hard.

Still, it must be remembered that this intellectual strife, like the physical strife in which the world is now engaged, is only a means to that "good life" of the philosophers and is not "the good life" itself. That life is growth to power through contemplation of beauty, whether beauty of body, of mind, or of soul. Beauty should be as natural a property of a city as of a poem, and of a civilization as of a statue. It is a quality of government as well as of art, of social intercourse as well as of music. With it, however the joyous highway of our lives may be streaked with the shadows of sorrow; we should breathe at all times an atmosphere of delight. Without it we are unworthy to enjoy the splendours of the sunrise and the sunset, the grandeur of the mountains and the sea, and show ourselves mere drones set to toil at paving the way for the advent of a more illustrious race.

It is in contemplation of beauty that we realize the fullness of life and demonstrate our right to walk this planet with heads erect as lords of the visible existence. That contemplation is no mere idleness. It entails an intense and constant activity to create beauty where it is not, and to fight with and clear away ugliness that we may render beauty visible where it already is. All our social action, whether political, military, literary, artistic, scientific or economic in its nature,

---

[15] See Rupert Brooke's "Peace" (1914).

must, to justify it, have this in view—the growth in power and beauty of the soul of man. Whatever the politicians and economists may say, it is for this end that great wars like this war, are fought, and for this end wounds and death are a small price.

(1917)

Appendix B: Canadian Authors Writing about World War I Poetry

Canadians were not only writing poetry about the war, they were also writing about war poetry and explaining its quantity, merits, and functions. The following selections give voice to a variety of perspectives of the war poetry. John Ridington's account is at once suspicious about and fond of this poetry. In his view, it is hampered by circumstance, but at the same time it provides a much needed inspirational document of the war. Logan's preface treats war poetry as a valuable record of what men thought and saw in the trenches and a vehicle for high-minded ideals of truth and beauty. Finally, the excerpt from Scott reminds us that one of the popular topics of pre-war poetry—nature—provided a necessary escape from wartime conditions.

John Ridington,[1] *The Poetry of War: An Address Delivered Before the Pacific Northwest Library Association at the Public Library, Portland, Oregon, September 5, 1917.* [Vancouver?], [1918?].

The difficulty of keeping abreast of the literature of his time, of which the wisest of kings complained, was a mere trifle by comparison with the task the printed page imposes on present day readers. To be widely and accurately informed on even one subject of general interest is impossible, when there are but twenty-four hours in a day, and sleeping, eating, and earning a living occupy all but a few of them. The literature of the Great War is a conclusive example of this. Messrs. Lange and Berry's annotated list,[2] published less than six months after the outbreak, showed hundreds of books on the struggle, and in

---

[1] In 1917, John Ridington was University of British Columbia's Acting Librarian and delivered this address at the Pacific Northwest Library Association meeting on 5 September 1917. Ridington certainly was not alone in noting the sheer quantity of war literature in the Western world. What is unique, however, is his explanation of the poetry's quality.

[2] Frederick William Theodor Lange and W. Turner Berry, *Books on the Great War: An Annotated Bibliography of Literature Issues During the European Conflict* (London: Grafton, 1915).

addition, over fifty entries under "Poetry, Songs and Plays," seventy volumes of "Sermons, Hymns and Prayers," twenty of "Humour," and more than a score of histories. When, to this beginning, is added the ever increasing and on-rushing volumes inundating us every month, and the scores of thousands of magazine articles, one realizes the futility of any effort to keep step with a literature that in forty months is in a position to mock any attempt at successful assimilation.

This is true, not only of the literature of the war as a whole, but also of its poetry. A Munich professor, replying to the charge of enemies, such at Maeterlinck and Vaerhaven, that his is a nation of barbarians, in disproof of the accusation triumphantly asserted that in the first five months of the cataclysm Germany had written 3,000,000 poems! Schumann, in his book "Germany and the World War," says 6,000,000 poems were produced in the first year of the war! Whether or not that be true, the output makes the hardiest of readers blench. More than three hundred volumes of verses have been written, with some phase of the war as the entire subject. A dozen anthologies have been issued, and more are in preparation. "The Poets' Corner" of every newspaper contains fugitive verse on the war, and some of it worthy of permanent preservation. War verse dominates in the magazines. The human aspirations and passions, the emotional analyses and manifestations that, with the visible and natural world, constitute the basic poetic material, today are seen through, and colored by, the red mists that enwrap all civilization.

This is inevitable. Literature is Life, and Poetry, Passion. Confronted by Armageddon, with personal, social, national, racial ideals of liberty imperilled, men think deeply, feel acutely, react powerfully. It would be unthinkable that this reaction should not find vent in poetry, the most permanent of all the great avenues of human expression.

It is a popular, but mistaken, expectation that great events necessarily produce great poetry. [...] And the present war, though it has produced an enormous bulk of poetry, much of it good, some of it excellent, has produced little that promises to be immortal. There are several reasons for this. Foremost among them has been placed the vastness, the immensity, the complexity of the struggle. It is not merely a life and death conflict of millions upon millions of men, fighting on a dozen fronts, in fertile farmlands, in arid deserts, on snowy steppes. These innumerable hosts are fighting in the heavens above, on the earth beneath, and in the waters under the earth fighting not only with weapons of hitherto unimagined destructive power, and of unbelievable precision and ingenuity, but also with weapons as primitive as those used by the Philistines and Romans, and with adaptations of the plate armour of medieval knights. They are fighting each other with the science of the bacteriologist and of the chemist, with disease germs, flame, and chlorine gases. [...] Wives and mothers are planning economical meals, and thus by serving in the national army of conservation are as truly "doing their bit" as their Red Cross sisters in hospital ward and dressing station. A thousand forces—military and naval, social and financial, industrial and economic—are inextricably interwoven in this war. Their ramifications have such interrelations and reactions that they affect, if not personally and directly, at least subconsciously, the most humdrum and prosaic lives. With us in Canada war has become the normal condition, to which we instinctively and automatically adjust our personal and communal lives. In future days these conditions will be studied and set forth by historians, economists and psychologists, but, in the mass, they cannot be set forth by poetry. Poetry seeks and insists upon the personal, the dramatic, elements of life. This vast, machine[-]made war dwarfs the merely personal: no cycle of human experience can comprehend or include its immensities. At best a poem can but reflect a single and minute facet from the blood red ruby of war. From the gigantic task of depicting it as a whole, in all its horror and heroism, its sacrifice and tragedy, its degradation, exaltation, purification, the Muses shrink back, appalled, shuddering, impotent.

Perhaps, too, the poets, in common with the rest of mankind, are too near to see or sense its titanic perspectives. All feel themselves mere human atoms engulfed in a madly swirling maelstrom, incapable of aught but blind struggle for the preservation of the interests and ideals they hold dear, incapable of striking deeper notes than those of vehemence and outraged sensibility. Wordsworth said of

poetry that it was emotion, remembered in tranquility.[3] Who can—
who would be tranquil now? [...]

To this generally accepted reason for the comparative infrequency
with which really excellent poetry has appeared under the stimulus of
the War, should be added another, in my opinion equally important.
Nationalism is passing away: the era of internationalism has not only
dawned, it has brightened almost into day. Patriotism in its old
sense—that of love for a geographical locality or historical sequence
of events—has been gradually dying as a motive stimulus to
men. [...] We should be thankful for the sense of humor that prevents
this. The traveled man is always the most tolerant; he whose life
centers about the parish pump is ever the most willing to think the
worst of nations he has never seen. But patriotic poetry, as we read it
in our school-books, stresses—indeed, deals almost wholly with the
history and achievements of a particular people, living in a particular
place, and, at least by implication, asserts that that people are great and
good and glorious because certain among them were heroic. [...]

The verse of the soldier poets will be remembered, some of it
longer even than their valiant deeds. Some of them hide their serious-
ness in laughter, some call like clarions to constancy and courage—
all to duty, faith, service. They rebuke our flippancy, our indifference,
our selfishness, our materialism. From the heavens above, and the
waters under the earth: from the seas they sweep in triumph, the lines
they hold, the fields they conquer, they call to us at home to do and
to endure. Many of them "poured out the red wine of youth, gave up
the years to be of comfort and of joy."[4] From little wooden crosses in
shell-torn, shot-swept countrysides they point us back to another,
that in even greater darkness was once set on

> "a green hill, far away,
> Without a city wall:"[5]

In these days of stress and peril to civilization and humanity, the
poets, soldier or civilian, are fulfilling their mission. They are still the

---

[3] See William Wordsworth's Preface to *Lyrical Ballads* (1802).
[4] See Rupert Brooke's "The Dead" (1915).
[5] See Cecil Frances Alexander's "There Is a Green Hill Far Away" (1847).

seers, champions, consolers, inspirers of mankind. They voice our prayers, our hopes. They cry to us of Freedom, Truth, Sacrifice. They have reborn in us a poignant consciousness of the reality, the everlasting spiritual preciousness, of ideals for which men gladly die. [...]

(1917)

John Daniel Logan. Preface to *The New Apocalypse and Other Poems of Days and Deeds in France.* Halifax: T.C. Allen, 1919. xi–xvi, 31–37.

The Soldier-Poet—the fighting poet—a song on his lips, a sword in his hand—is no new social phenomenon. King David of Israel[6] is to the modern heart the prototype of the lyrical warrior. Aeschylus,[7] Tyrtaeus[8] and Simoniedes[9] were the outstanding soldier-poets of Greece in ancient times. Dante,[10] in mediaeval days, was a soldier-poet. In the century preceding our own, Byron[11] and Walt Whitman[12] were authentic poets who fought or served in the field. In short, all wars have produced, or have had, their soldier-poets. But the late Great War, in this regard, differs memorably and uniquely from other wars, in at least three important ways. First, the number of soldier-poets in general and actually produced in the field by the Great War is a phenomenon by itself: an army of singers in an army of warriors. Secondly, the excellence of the poetry, much of it produced in the field to the awful and Hadean[13] accompaniment of screaming shell and thunderous artillery, is also a phenomenon by itself. Thirdly, the flowering of the poetic spirit on the fighting field has, by admiration and emulation, not only

---

[6]   Musician, poet, ruler, and soldier in the Bible, David is said to have defeated Goliath, written a number of psalms, and been anointed King of Israel; see especially 1 Samuel 16:14–23.

[7]   Playwright in ancient Greece and soldier at the Battle of Marathon.

[8]   Elegiac poet in ancient Greece, whose poems are typically about war, death, and heroism; also participant in the Second Messenian War.

[9]   Ancient Greek poet of elegies, lyrics, and epigrams.

[10]   Italian poet, member of the cavalry in the Battle of Campaldino, and (more famously) author of *The Divine Comedy* (1321).

[11]   English lyric poet who, in his later years, sailed to Greece to aid in their struggles with Turkey.

[12]   American poet (famously of *Leaves of Grass* [1855]) and participant in the American Civil War.

[13]   of Hades, the underworld (Greeky mythology)

stimulated the general poetic spirit but also caused it to disclose its existence and potency in a new generation of poets of nature, society and the arts of peace. In a phrase, the Great War has created an authentic Renascence[14] of the Poetic Spirit and of Poetry.

I shall say a few words about each of these singular results of the late war. As to number, the fact is that the total of poets, lay and martial, inspired by all the wars of the past are not nearly so many as are the strictly so-called soldier-poets inspired or produced by the recent Great War. The creative poetic spirit in the armies of the Allied Nations was as universal and democratic as the fighting spirit: the outburst of song in the field issued from the hearts of all ranks; officers, as well as n.c.o.'s[15] and men, were alike spontaneously, under inward compulsion, moved to utter the thoughts and emotions which they found welling up in their consciousness and hearts when facing the tremendous realities of their new and overwhelmingly obsessing experiences of the greater love and of war and death. That the poetic spirit should be so universally manifested in the Allied armies, particularly in the armies of the British, which includes those of the Overseas Dominions, was due, no doubt, to the fact that there was never before in any other fighting bodies of troops so many men of education and culture, gifted to become poets under adequate inspiration, and so many men who, previous to the war, successfully essayed verse and poetry, as were even in the ranks of the armies of the Allied peoples.

What is, however, significant is not the number of the soldier-poets inspired or produced by the Great War but the *excellence* of their poetry—an excellence both of *ideas* and of *artistic form*. The truth is that only in the verse of the soldier-poets shall we see clearly, vividly, as if transfigured in the skies, what men really think and feel about war and death and love and home and country and the good green earth and peace. Sincerity and truth may be found in the verse of other poets; but sincerity and truth of ideas are the very life and

---

[14]   rebirth; also a period of literary history from 1500–1660 in England (Abrams)
[15]   non-commissioned officers

soul of the verse of the soldier-poets inspired by the Great War. In closest contact with Reality, these soldier-poets sang of truth for their own comfort, solace, strengthening and joy in noble doing—and they sang beautifully; and because they sang nobly and beautifully, their poetry became solace to the broken-hearts, support to the fainting, and spiritual refreshment, in Satan's despite, to the undaunted and unconquerable before the hosts of Satan. As soldiers they gave the world noble examples of manliness, fortitude and self-sacrifice. As poets they gave the world great ideas and emotions, some of them transfigured with art that is beautiful and others of them flaming with undying splendour.

Truth, beauty and splendour—these are the three supreme excellences of the poetry written on active service, on the fighting field, by the soldier-poets inspired by the late Great War. I must, however, remove a misapprehension. The wonder is that their poetry could have any excellence, formal or spiritual, at all, if we consider that the most of it was scribbled down on any bits of paper to hand, and scribbled at chance times and places, and not only under all sorts of discouragements, impediments and interruptions but also to the accompaniment of the diapason[16] of the awful engines of death and while the poet himself could not know whether or not the next moment as he wrote might be his last on earth. To have written it all and to have given it even a decent degree of formal finish, under the unhappy and awful circumstances of conception and writing, must justly be considered a unique and wonderful literary feat. Despite the untoward conditions on the field, the astounding facts are that the verse of the soldier-poets, the verse actually written on the field or at least on active service, in many instances is on a high level of excellence in form and imagery, and that in a few instances it has attained to immortal beauty, glowing on the utmost verge of noble art with undying splendour. I have, therefore, no patience with, and certainly no respect for, those fatuous critics who refuse to apply the epithet "great" to the war-verse of the soldier-poets, on the ground that, as

---

[16]   musical notes separated by an octave

the critics allege, it has not the formal finish expected in sustained production. It is all, as I said, in the nature of a literary feat, and done by young poets under the most untoward or harrowing circumstances; and though much of it lacks the finish of perfect art, the best of it is *great in ideas*. [...]

They left, moreover, a legacy of inspiration. Admiration for the verse of the soldier-poets has resulted in a noticeable revival of the creative poetic spirit. Their fine and noble work in poetry has caused a new conception of the spiritual dignity and office of the true, that is, the sincere, poet. The inspiration is derived from the reflection that if the poetry of the soldier-poets was so potent for noble vision, for moral impetus, for solace, for spiritual sustenance or refreshment, and for absolute loyalty to the ideal, and if it was written, as it was, under the most untoward circumstances and yet written with as much concern as possible for ideas and formal finish, then, inasmuch as these soldier-poets achieved so splendidly as they did in poetry, how much more should poets who can write, at leisure and in peace, be obedient to the highest ideals of nobility in conception and of beauty in artistry and craftsmanship whenever they essay poetry. If the living poets do not obey the voice of the fallen soldier-poets, the work of these soldier-poets shall rise up in judgement against them—and condemn them. [...]

I cannot close this Preface without a few explanatory words about the Dedication.[17] It may strike some minds as too exclusive. It may be inquired why I did not include the Wives and Sweethearts, along with the Mothers. Let me say that all the prose and verse which I wrote while overseas, in camp or in the line, and which was published in the Canadian press—and I wrote considerable—was composed and published for the sustaining and comforting of the Mothers, Wives, Sisters, and Sweethearts of my gallant comrades in the 85th Battalion, Nova Scotia Highlanders. I have, however, in the Dedication to the

---

[17]   The dedication reads, "To the Mothers Of My Martyred Comrades Who Fell on The Field of Honor, 1917, 1918,—Whose Dust Has Hallowed the Soil of France and of Flanders, and Whose Sacrificial Death Has Wrought For Humanity A New Atonement!"

little volume in hand, special reasons for memorializing THE MOTHERS of my beloved fallen companions in arms. I have helped, in the line while shells screamed and artillery roared and wrought destruction of human life nearby, to wrap many of my fallen comrades in their last blanket and lay them in their last earthly resting place. Living soldiers' tears and prayers at the rude obsequies over the remains of fallen comrades were a poor substitute for mothers' last tears and the last kiss of eternal love. Still, we who ministered at the obsequies always thought of the mothers at the burial of comrades— we thought of them chiefly—and gave our fallen companions the best substitute we could give in the stead of mothers' tears and farewells. Moreover, I have never heard from mortally wounded and dying comrades—and many of them were mere lads, and no doubt some of them were, in that dear, homely term of affection, "the baby" boys of their families—I have never heard from the dying a whimper of regret, but I have heard—oh, the tender pathos of it!—from lips soon to be sealed in silence forever the low, faint call, barely more than a whisper, "Mamma, mamma, mamma." Any psychologist will say that this was inevitable. As the earliest expressions of love which these fallen, dying soldiers experienced were those of mother-love and care, so, naturally, in the dissolution of spirit from body, the last call of these passing heroes was the human call for the mothers who bore them and to whom they, in the days before their manhood, turned for love, comforting and strengthening. [...]

(1919)

From Frederick George Scott, *The Great War As I Saw It.* Toronto: Goodchild, 1922.

I went down the steep steps into a long dark passage, lit here and there by the light which came from the rooms on either side. The whole place was crowded with men and the atmosphere was more than usually thick. I made my way down to the end where there was a pump which had been put there by the Germans. Here the men were filling their water-bottles, and I got a fresh supply for mine. Not far from the pump a few steps led down into a room where I found the C.O. and a number of the officers of the 1st Battalion. It was about two a.m., and they were having a breakfast of tea and bacon and invited me to join them. After the meal was finished, the Colonel, who was lying on a rough bed, said to me, "Sit down, Canon, and give us some of your nature poems to take our minds off this beastly business." It was very seldom that I was invited to recite my own poems, so such an opportunity could not be lost. I sat down on the steps and repeated a poem which I wrote among the Laurentian mountains, in the happy days before we ever thought of war. It is called, "The Unnamed Lake."[18]

There is not much in the poem, but, like a gramophone record, it carried our minds away into another world. For myself, who remembered the scenery that surrounded me when I wrote it and who now, in that filthy hole, looked at the faces of young men who in two or three hours were to brave death in one of the biggest tasks that had been laid upon us, the words stirred up all sorts of conflicting emotions.

The recitation seemed to be so well received that I ventured on another—in fact several more—and then I noticed a curious thing. It was the preternatural silence of my audience. Generally speaking, when I recited my poems, one of the officers would suddenly remember he had to dictate a letter, or a despatch rider would come in with orders. Now, no one stirred. I paused in the middle of a poem and looked round to see what was the matter, and there to my astonishment, I found that everyone, except the young Intelligence Officer, was sound asleep. It was the best thing that could have happened and I secretly consoled myself with the reflection that the one who was unable to sleep was the officer who specialized in intelligence. We both laughed quietly, and then I whispered to him, "We had better go and find some place where we, too, can get a little rest." He climbed over the prostrate forms and followed me down the passage to a little excavation where the Germans had started to make a new passage. We

---

[18] The poem appears in Scott's *The Unnamed Lake and Other Poems* (1897).

lay down side by side on the wooden floor, and I was just beginning to succumb to the soothing influences of my own poetry, when I thought I felt little things crawling over my face. It was too much for me. I got up and said, "I think I am getting crummy, so I'm going off." I looked in on the General and the Brigade Major, and then climbed up the steps and went to the machine-gun hut.

(1922)

Appendix C: Perspectives on Canadian War Art: A Case Study

The Canadian War Memorials Fund sponsored British and Canadian artists in their efforts to record war experiences otherwise unattended to or in ways never before seen. Diverse in style (from traditional to avant-garde, from Romantic to Modernist, from naturalist to abstract) and topic (from the home front to the front lines, from munitions factories to bomb-torn battlefields), the over four hundred works of art were thought—by politicians, critics, and viewers—to be a much-needed memorial of the war efforts, its participants, and its consequences.

In its first showing in London, the collection was received enthusiastically, so enthusiastically in fact that by the time it reached Canada, it was known as "The Art Sensation of the World." And while most of the reviews at home were as glowing as the ones from across the Atlantic, their subtle differences reveal some of the prevailing attitudes about war art, what it should look like and what it should do. For British art critic Paul Konody, the war was a chance to memorialize the war and, at the same time, acknowledge recent artistic innovations. But the anonymous reviews in the *Toronto World* and *Star Weekly* were more suspicious of the new art's ability to give an accurate and effective interpretation of the war. These debates about the form and function of war art were not limited to the Canadian War Memorials collection, and can help us understand the early and enduring responses to the period's poetry.

Paul Konody, "On War Memorials." *Art and War: Canadian War Memorials, A Selection of the Works Executed for the Canadian War Memorials Fund to Form a Record of Canada's Part in the Great War and a Memorial to those Canadians Who Have Made the Great Sacrifice.* **London: Canadian War Memorials Office, 1919. 5–16.**[1]

"Great nations," says Ruskin[2] in his preface to "St. Mark's Rest," "write their autobiographies in three manuscripts:—the book of their deeds, the book of their words, and the book of their art. Not one of these books can be understood unless we read the two others; but of the three the only quite trustworthy one is the last. The acts of a nation may be triumphant by its good fortune, and its words mighty by the genius of a few of its children, but its art only by the general gifts and common sympathies of the race."

One might go further than Ruskin and say that the book of a nation's deeds would be meaningless, or at least undecipherable, without the book of art which supplies the needed key. The book of art is older even than the book of words. To the book of art we have to refer for our knowledge of the earliest civilizations. As we turn its leaves, we read of the rise and fall of mighty Empires, of social and political institutions, of great individual achievements, and above all, of the wars that play so dominant a part in the history of the nations. For war, or rather victory, has always had a stimulating effect upon artistic production; and many of the triumphs of early art that have been saved from the destruction wrought by time or by the hand of man, are commemorative of war-like achievements: they may, indeed, be regarded as war memorials. Moreover, the book of art is more reliable than the book of words. Not that the artist was less prone to exaggerate than the chronicler, or less given to flattery of the powers that employed him. But the historian, as a rule, was too much absorbed in *events* to trouble about the daily life, the appearance, the

---

[1] British art critic Paul Konody (1872–1933) wrote the introduction to the collection's guide book.
[2] John Ruskin (1819–1900), an influential English artist and critic.

surroundings of the pawns on the chess-board of history. There was no need for him to describe what to him was obvious. A war, for instance, means to him statistics, strategic and tactical movements and their results, treaties and alliances, and the glory of individual rulers or generals. The sculptor and the painter, on the other hand, have to visualize their subject and build it up of those material details which the chronicler scarcely touches upon, as being too obvious, but which, in their ensemble, constitute the life and civilization of a period [...].

When the idea was conceived to provide Canada with a War Memorial to keep before the eyes of future generations a complete pictorial record of the Dominion's sacrifices and achievements in the great war, the organisers of the scheme were faced with considerable difficulties. Not the least of these was the extraordinary complexity of the material that had to be dealt with, if the record was to comprise every phase of a war that was fought not only on land on three continents, but on the sea, under the sea, in the air, and, more than on any previous occasion, on what has been aptly called the home front. The work in munition factories and dockyards, in training camp and hospital, in the lumber camps and on the land, in aviation works and in camouflage ateliers,[3] on railway and on road, was as important as the fighting activity at the front. To do complete justice to all these phases was obviously an impossibility. The most that could be done was to select a few typical scenes of every kind of war work, which would show the progress from the earliest stages of preparation to the more exciting happenings in the trenches and on the battlefields. The second consideration was of a purely aesthetic nature: how to maintain some kind of homogeneity in so comprehensive a scheme, whilst avoiding the deadly monotony of the dull array of battle pictures which line the endless walls of the Palace at Versailles, which is as depressing as the clash and confusion of the haphazard gatherings of the ordinary picture gallery. Conditions to-day are vastly different from those prevailing in the golden days of the Renaissance,

---

[3]   workshops, usually for artists

when a master-painter could with a light heart undertake the fresco decoration of entire churches or monasteries. He was the head of a *bottega*,[4] and had under him a small army of trained assistants who worked under his direction in his own manner. If he died before the work was completed, another master, trained in the same tradition, could take it up and carry it to a successful conclusion. [...]

To-day the *bottega* system has become obsolete. We live in an age of individualism, and nowhere is this more pronounced than in art. In painting, the present condition is nothing short of chaotic. Apart from the men who stand outside all groups, we have academic painters, realists, naturalists, plein-airists, impressionists, neo-realists, neo-impressionists, expressionists, cubists, vorticists, futurists, representative of every step leading from strictly representational to abstract art. To make the collection of memorial paintings truly representative of the artistic outlook during the momentous period of the great war, examples of all these conflicting tendencies had to be included. A completely homogenous plan, like the great decorative enterprises of the Renaissance could not be thought of. The aim was bound to be diversity rather than uniformity, but diversity kept under control, with a definite end in view. This end was, that the principal pictures should maintain a certain unity of scale and decorative treatment which would make them suitable to take their place in a specially designed architectural setting, the smaller paintings and sketches being left to be arranged in groups in the various galleries provided for this purpose. A carefully organised decorative scheme was thus to be supplemented by a comprehensive pictorial record. A balance was to be maintained between the historical and the aesthetic aspects. [...]

(1918)

---

[4] "Artist's workshop" (Italian).

Anonymous, "War's Spirit in Painter's Colors." *The Toronto World*, August 27, 1919.

Land and Ocean Contribute Grim Tragedies of Carnage Past—"THE FLAG"—Byam Shaw's Allegory Leaves Lasting Impression on Every Beholder

Four different catalogs are required to describe the art and war memorials in the great Exhibition, and these four collections, the war relics, the war paintings, the Canadian art exhibit and the photographic collection, there is sufficient material to occupy the visitor for several days. For those whose time is more limited a few notes may not be out of place. In the regular art gallery of the Exhibition is to be found the "war memorials exhibition," consisting of pictures by Canadian artists sent to the front and others in the ranks, and by other artists of non-Canadian birth. The eminent London critic, Mr. Konody, is in charge of the collection, and is most courteous in affording information. Of the pictures and portraits there will be many differing views, if the standards of art be taken into consideration, but it will be wiser for the casual visitor to ignore questions of this kind and judge the pictures with certain exceptions, on a basis of information. They are intended as a record. In this respect by far the largest number of pictures are from the brush of Lieut. A.Y. Jackson, A.R.C.A., and, on the whole, they are a very satisfactory series. Lieut. Cyril H. Barraud, Lieut. Alfred Bastien, Capt. Maurice Cullen, R.C.A.; Capt. R.G. Matthews, Lieut. H.J. Mowat, A.J. Munnings, Private A. Nantel, Lieut. Paul Nash, C.R.W. Nevinson, Leonard Richmond, R.B.A., Lieut. Gyrth Russell, are the other more frequent contributors. There are a great many portraits, both of living and dead. Several of the Canadian V.C.'s are depicted. The most notable omission, which can scarcely be excused in Toronto, is that of Major-General Mercer.

"The Flag"
Of the pictures that excite universal comment, Byam Shaw's great work, "The Flag," probably leaves the most lasting impression. It is

intelligible to every class of observer. The dead soldier lying in the relentless clutch of the grim monster of war is the centre of interest of a representative group of every class of humanity, the young, the old, the middle-aged, the rich, the poor, those of high rank and low, the toiler, the idler, the parent, the child, the lover, the friend, the servant. All are gripped in that terrible clutch. The expression varies on every face. Wonder, awe, reverence, fear, pity, horror, consternation, despair, faith, perplexity, resignation, love, peace, the world in little appears here, in such glorious art as raises no problems of color or medium or style. The master hand that produced it was still in death within a few weeks of completing this work.

Another splendid piece of work is "The Night Patrol—Canadian Motor Launch Boats Entering Dover," by Lieut. Julius Olsson, R.N.V.R., A.R.A. The oily tides of the channel glisten under the searchlights, and the sheets of foam mark the path where the swift boats have passed. The heaving mystery of the ocean has never been more powerfully indicated. [...]

The First Landing

[...] One hesitates in these days of revolution in art to say anything about many of the pictures that have come from the hands influenced by the new impulses and conceptions of drawing and color. The old idea used to be to give a faithful representation, and art was formerly regarded as being as logical as science or philosophy. The new art discards logic. For example, in the pictures of a munition factory the machinery and shells look in the picture exactly as they do in reality. The men and women, however, look like nothing in heaven above or the earth beneath, or in the waters under the earth as far as previous records go. One hesitates to think that Canadians looked like these creatures, even under the debilitating influence of the English climate.

We feel quite sure, however, that the visitor who takes the catalog and studies these 447 pictures will have learned a great deal more about our Canadian boys at the front, the conditions under which they fought, and lived, than in any other way.

(1919)

Anonymous, "More Shocks in Store for Ordinary Folk at 'Ex' Art Gallery." *Star Weekly*, August 20, 1920.

The public must be prepared for further shocks when it visits the art gallery at the Exhibition.

There are some war memorial paintings on show, and among them are a dozen or so of the "Modernist" school.

The *Star Weekly* was permitted a preliminary glimpse of the exhibit earlier this week and in the gallery we found Mr. P.G. Konody, the eminent English art critic of the "London Observer," who is in charge of the war memorial paintings for Canada.

The prize piece of modernism is a canvas about as big as a shop window entitled "Night Bombardment." This stupendous work is reproduced herewith.

Mr. Konody was very kind in his effort to elucidate this and the dozen of examples of modern art which are going to puzzle sorely several hundred thousand Canadians in the next two weeks. These paintings are for the decoration of a National war memorial building at Ottawa which will contain for posterity a record of the late war.

Woe, Woe, Posterity!

Mr. Konody said:

"This is abstract art. For hundreds of years, artists have been labouring in a false direction. Artists now are freeing themselves and are expressing their emotions in color, form and line; not merely reproducing as seen."

The National War Museum will be a temple of emotion.

At first sight, this canvas entitled "Night Bombardment" creates no emotion. It is a dull, dark green in general color. Bang in the middle is a stiff pyramid of starched valenciennes lace. There are several wavy circles in the foreground and along the horizon, if one speaks of the horizon in modern art, is a white irregular streak representing no doubt the smoke and light that dances on No Man's Land.

Mr. Konody said that this picture is the finest example of modern abstract art in the exhibition. The pyramid of lace represents a flare.

"Abstract," according to the dictionary, means "considered or conceived apart from its concrete or material nature."

"Night Bombardment" is indeed an abstract bombardment. It may represent the emotion of an artist on seeing a night bombardment. But everybody is not an artist.

After Mr. Konody had left us, and as we wandered about this empty gallery, we encountered two workmen engaged in cleaning up the gallery.

Both were returned soldiers and were snatching a few moments to look over the many fine and more appreciable pictures of old remembered scenes.

"There's Villers O Bo!" declared one, excitedly. "There's the house where mamzelle lived who did the laundry!"

"Hey, Joe!" called the other.

"Lookat here: darned if it isn't the old Pylones trench in front of Vimy!"

They had not, as yet, noticed the modernist works.

We joined them.

"What," we asked, after a while, "do you think of this?"

And we halted in front of "Night Bombardment."

Neither spoke. They gazed at it earnestly and respectfully.

"That," we said, "is a picture of a night bombardment."

After a surprised and closer inspection, the one said:

"Joe, by jingo, it does look like a little evening hate we saw that night we stole the officer's water bottle full of rum! Look! all bleary, and wavy and pink and purple! Wow! I'll bet the fellow who painted this one has a fine large night to remember. I wonder if it was our company officers he was visiting by any chance?"

Turning to us, he asked:

"What is that white painted thing in the middle?"

"A flare. A verey light."[5]

"That settles it, Joe," said the soldier. "It was our company officers this artist was calling on when he painted that."

There were several other abstract pictures we inspected. One shows the Canadian Tunnelers making a tunnel. It is a huge canvas full of square beams, square hands, square faces, square men.

---

[5]   light produced by a flare gun

"The artist," we explained to the troops, "has carried the sqaureness of his theme into the figures of the men. It represents his emotion on seeing the tunnelers at work."

"Well," said Joe, who was a quiet little Englishman, I've seen them tunnelling; and what struck me was not the resemblance of the men to the squareness of the beams, but their exceptional roundness in comparison to the beams around them. If this artist had painted a mass of square beams and a whole crew of men who looked like plum puddings and roly-polies and footballers, he would have painted a picture. This picture is not true."

Then we looked at "The Conquerors"[6]— a modernist painting of the Montreal highlanders marching down Arras roads. It is a bleak, grey, flat horrible picture of a section of Highlanders marching through a shattered desolation. The faces of these men are really magnificent. All the rest of the huge painting fades away, as you look at these faces one after another.

"This fellow," said the soldier, "has got somewhere. Now, this is true. Yes, sir, I'm sitting on the roadside, watching them go past. I can hear the clinking and squashing as they march. I can smell the chalk road. I can hear the thump of guns."

There is a splendid big canvas of the arrival of the Canadians at the Rhine. Nothing abstract about this. A hundred or even twenty years ago, this painting would have consisted of a group of gorgeous generals and colonels, standing magnificently with the Rhine castles in the background. But this picture for Canada's memorial hall shows a group of buck privates. They have arrived at the Rhine. And they have forthwith opened their haversacks and are commencing to distribute bully beef.

As we stood making a last survey of the gallery, the soldier Joe said:

"Those modern paintings mean nothing to me. I have never seen anything in the war that they remind me of. If I bring my wife here

---

[6] "The Conquerors" (1920) by Eric Kennington (1888–1960) was criticized by soon-to-be Governor General of Canada, Lord Tweedsmuir, who said that Kennington's work is "undescriptive" and "remote"; "[h]e might just as well paint his pictures at home." *Canvas of War*, eds. Laura Brandon and Dean F. Oliver (Toronto: Douglas McIntyre, 2000), 27.

and show her those pictures, it will give her no idea of what I want her to know. But these others—that one of the Ypres Salient, that of the bloody dead Germans lying cluttered in the sunken road; and all these little ones—that of the dead officer, lying with his face to the sky—those will give my wife a real idea of what the war was like. Pictures will not preserve the emotions of war. The best they can do is preserve the scenes of war."

"I think," added the other soldier, "I have had my legged pulled."

(1920)

Sources

Contents

CALL, F.O. *Acanthus and Wild Grape.* Toronto: McClelland & Stewart, 1920.

———. *In a Belgian Garden and Other Poems.* London: Erskine MacDonald, 1917.

CAMPBELL, WILFRED. *Langemarck & Other Poems.* Ottawa, 1918.

———. *Lyrics of Iron and Mist.* Ottawa, 1916.

———. *War Lyrics.* Ottawa, 1915.

COLEMAN, HELENA. *Marching Men: War Verses.* Toronto: J.M. Dent, 1917.

DRUMMOND, ALBERT WILLIAM. *Rhymes of a Hut-Dweller.* [Canada?], 1918.

DURIE, ANNA. *Our Absent Hero.* Toronto: Ryerson Press, 1920.

DURKIN, DOUGLAS LEADER. *The Fighting Men of Canada.* Toronto: McClelland & Stewart, 1918.

HALE, KATHERINE. *Grey-Knitting, and Other Poems.* Toronto: Briggs, 1914.

———. *The White Comrade.* Toronto: McClelland, Goodchild & Stewart, 1916.

LOGAN, JOHN DANIEL. *Insulters of Death and Other Poems of the Great Departure.* Halifax: L. Clyde Davidson, 1916.

———. *The New Apocalypse and Other Poems of Days and Deeds in France.* Halifax: T. C. Allen, 1919.

MACDONALD, WILSON. *The Girl Behind the Man Behind the Gun.* [Victoria?], [1915?].

———. *Song of the Prairie Land and Other Poems.* Toronto: McClelland & Stewart, 1918.

PRATT, E.J. *E.J. Pratt: Complete Poems.* Eds. Sandra Djwa and R.G. Moyles. 2 vols. Toronto: University of Toronto Press, 1989.

———. *Newfoundland Verse.* Toronto: Ryerson Press, 1923.

PREWETT, FRANK. *Collected Poems.* Ed. Robert Graves. Toronto: Cassel, 1964.

———. *Poems.* Richmond, England: Hogarth, 1921.

———. *Selected Poems of Frank Prewett*. Eds. Bruce Meyer and Barry Callaghan. Toronto: Exile, 1987.

———. *The Collected Poems of Sir Charles G.D. Roberts*. Ed. Desmond Pacey. Wolfville, NS: Wombat Press, 1985. 304.

SCOTT, FREDERICK GEORGE. *In the Battle Silences: Poems Written at the Front*. Toronto: Musson,1917.

SERVICE, ROBERT W. *Rhymes of a Red Cross Man*. Toronto: Barse & Hopkins, 1916.

SMITH, A.J.M. *The Complete Poems*. London, ON: Canadian Poetry Press, 2008.

The Complete Poems and Letters of E.J. Pratt: A Hypertext Edition. Eds. Sandra Djwa and Zailig Pollock. Trent University. January 2009. <http://www.trentu.ca/faculty/pratt/>.

TREHEARNE, BRIAN. "Two Letters from A.J.M. Smith to W.E. Collin." *Canadian Poetry: Studies, Documents, Reviews* 54 (2004): 76–96.

TROTTER, BERNARD FREEMAN. *A Canadian Twilight and Other Poems of War and Peace*. Toronto: McClelland, Goodchild & Stewart, 1917.

YARDLEY, M. JEANNE. "'The Bitterness and Greatness': Reading F.G. Scott's *The Great War As I Saw It*." *Studies in Canadian Literature* 16.1 (Spring 1995): 195–205.

Credits

Every effort has been made to determine and contact copyright owners. In the case of any omissions, the publisher will be pleased to make suitable acknowledgement in future editions.

Literary Credits

E.J. PRATT. E.J. Pratt's poems are from *E.J. Pratt: Complete Poems*, edited by Sandra Djwa and R.G. Moyles (University of Toronto Press © 1989). Reprinted with the permission of the publisher.

FRANK PREWETT. As holder of the copyright to the poems and letters of her father, Frank Prewett, Jane Youngs is happy to give permission for Joel Baetz to include them in his anthology of English-Canadian Great War poetry.

A.J.M. SMITH. "A Soldier's Ghost" is included with the permission of William Toye, literary executor for the estate of A.J.M. Smith.

Picture Credits

iii   Courtesy of Guelph Museums, McCrae House.
17   City of Toronto Archives, Fonds 1065, Series 833, File 2, id0005
34   Queen's Archives V009-PGc-260
44   Victoria University Library
55   Library and Archives Canada / C-006718
59   Courtesy of the William Ready Division of Archives and Research Collections, McMaster University Library
63   Miscellaneous / Library and Archives Canada / C-003187
72   Vaughan Memorial Library Special Collections, Acadia University
80   Courtesy of Guelph Museums, McCrae House
83   Library and Archives Canada / PA-110158
111   Victoria University Library
121   University of Manitoba Archives & Special Collections
141   Courtesy of the William Ready Division of Archives and Research Collections, McMaster University Library